Proceeds from this book will be donated to:

Center for Advanced Medicine at Siteman Cancer Center
BJC Health Care
Saint Louis, Missouri

ISBN: 9798218933029

All song lyrics reprinted with permission from Jenny Kavanaugh and Neko Case

Cover design and book layout by Victoria Brzustowicz, victoriabcreative.com

Front and Back Cover Photo: Sunrise over the Mississippi River in Chester, Illinois

For Liam, Ken, Kevin, Linda, and Debbie. John loved his family. You filled his heart with joy. Thank you for the love and happiness you brought into his life.

For Mary. John loved you like his own mother. Thank you for teaching me from an early age how to be a caregiver even though I didn't know what I was learning or why I was learning it.

For Ana. You take care of all God's creatures. I couldn't have gotten through this without you. Thank you for always showing up.

For Dr. Chris Beuer. You and your staff were a godsend for John in his last months. I don't have words to express how grateful I am for you and each and every angel in your office. Thank you for your commitment to this special vocation.

For Jen. Your music inspires me. Your reason in the midst of chaos sustains me. Thank you for being a great friend and neighbor to both John and me. Your frequent presence eased John's pain and made our days a little brighter.

For my amazing editor and new professional literary friend, John Ryan. Language is powerful. You helped me focus my words, and you helped me get this baby out of the womb and into the world. I learned so much from you and am so thankful for your guidance. You are an extraordinary teacher.

Love,
John

Photo of John, 2015, waiting for the Patty Griffin show to start

Bill Waggoner

Story Guide

Foreword

by Jen Kavanaugh

The house on the corner was the place to be.

When I first met Bill, he lived in an old brick building at the end of the block. I liked him immediately- he is straightforward and honest with a great sense of humor. He suffers no fools.

Not long after meeting Bill, I met John, who was similar to Bill in some ways — quick to laugh and difficult to shock. Bill will be the first to tell you, however, that John was "nicer." John had an unmistakable openness about him. He loved to talk to people and would listen with such a connectedness that he immediately felt like a friend. And he was the perfect foil for Bill, who would occasionally, or mostly, veer into an always funny snark while John would slowly shake his head with a wry smile.

Together, they were pretty close to perfect.

A few years after I met Bill, he and John bought a different house, across the street from the first. They made a wonderful home together — both literally and figuratively. Their home was beautifully designed and decorated, with compelling art, stylish retro furniture, and music always playing through excellent speakers. The lighting was perfect, and your favorite cocktail could be whipped up in minutes. The most appealing part of the home, of course, was John and Bill themselves. They were the consummate hosts. With them, you were sure to laugh, and if you were to delve into deeper, more personal conversational territory, Bill would provide a healthy dose of straight-to-the-point observations, while John found ways to make you feel like he was your personal cheerleader. All of this while Neko Case sang in the background as you sipped your gin and tonic. It took me a long time — years, in fact — to realize that in order to make sure a guest felt welcome they would rarely, if ever, let them know when it was time to leave. And it was often difficult to leave, when you were in such a lovely place with such lovely company.

It seems almost crazy when I say this now, but that hardly changed when John got sick. They still hosted — often. Their house always seemed to be bustling with the excitement of dinner parties and neighborhood happy hours. And they were much the same — affable, clever, and thoughtful. I often had to remind myself that John had to have been feeling terrible much of the time, as a result of his various treatment protocols, and force myself to leave when I noticed him sneak a yawn. But for the most part, to many who knew them, not much seemed different.

Of course, for the two of them, almost everything had changed. Every minute of John's day was spent coping with his illness or the side effects of the treatments. And their relationship shifted in small, then monumental ways as John's illness progressed. When John was first diagnosed, and it was clear they had tough days ahead of them, it was difficult to imagine both of these deeply independent individuals having to adapt to a relationship that included caregiving. For the entirety of their relationship to that point they had lived in separate houses, with separate schedules, and even separate friend groups, to an extent. At every new turn of the illness, I imagined how frustrated John must have been to have lost yet more autonomy, and how confining it had to be for Bill, who eventually would have every hour of every day tied to the care that John required. I never heard either one of them openly complain about these struggles. The frustrations were only alluded to through humor, as they seemed to share the philosophy that the physical and emotional pain they were experiencing would not be alleviated by dwelling on it.

The social aspect of who they were was one thing they could try to keep constant, and in many ways, it became a lifeline and an outlet for them both. John loved to be with friends and family, and Bill loved to see John happy. So, they continued to host, even in the midst of doctor appointments, chemo, radiation, and for John, tremendous amounts of pain.

I am certain that every couple's journey through an illness is unique, and I had never been a close part of such a journey, like I was with John and Bill. I can say that it was a remarkable thing to observe, as they faced every twist and turn with honesty and grace. I saw both of my dear friends shift and adapt to painful new realities, and it revealed that they were exactly who they always were. They were open and funny. Bill would say all of the true things, and John would somehow turn the gaze of every conversation away from his own struggles so he could listen to and support everyone else. They listened together, finished each other's sentences, and always asked you to stay for dinner. They laughed a lot. My favorite thing was listening to them tell a story together. They shared so many stories of their many years together, of the wild experiences they had and unique characters they met along the way, and when they got into the flow, Bill would add a one-liner, John would laugh, each would add little bits here and there, speaking in tandem, filling in details… it was wonderful.

This is one more wonderful story of John and Bill. It provides a glimpse into their unique experience, told with candor and love. And while Bill does most of the heavy lifting on this one, it is most definitely their story, and when I read it, I can hear John's voice on every page.

184 Days

Everybody has a story. This is John's. And this is mine.

Today I write. It's been one-hundred and eighty-four days since John left us. Six or eight times over the last four years I've started. Then I'd quit. Maybe I didn't have anything to say. Unlikely. Or maybe I couldn't face it. Most likely. But I always stopped. This time I don't want to stop. I don't want to stop because, now, I'm afraid I'm going to forget. I just don't want to forget. I don't want to forget him. I don't want to forget John.

Relationships are hard. Navigating those choppy waters is challenging enough without a chaotic terminal diagnosis trying to toss you overboard and drag you under. John and I started dating in the summer of 2003. We had a group of mutual friends. He had gone through a divorce and had a five-year-old son. I knew "of" John, and I also knew his ex-wife. I remember the first time I talked to him at a party. I said to myself that this was the person I wanted to spend the rest of my life with. He had never been in a same-sex relationship before. But we just had that connection. For the next 21 years, we did it all together. *Except* live together. Until we had to.

People say that things happen for a reason. I'm not so sure about that. I don't know why good things happen. I don't know why bad things happen. I don't know why people are lucky or unlucky. Maybe things just happen because they do. John lived in a historic suburb of St. Louis, and I lived in the city. Most of the things we did were in the city. Because John had shared custody of his son, Liam, and he was five when we started dating, neither of us were in a huge hurry to cohabitate. Logistically, it was easier for Liam to stay where he was, which was also close to his mom. Neither of us were threatened by living apart. And we spent a good three or four nights a week together. I often say the secret to a successful relationship is maintaining two separate households.

For the first sixteen years we were together, I lived in a very tall, 1890s Victorian storefront mixed-use building that I had converted into a single-family residence. Originally, a grocery store was on the first floor, and the owner's living quarters were on the second floor. It was a great "loft-esque" space, but the ceilings on the first floor were twelve feet tall. The staircase to the second story was a killer. I'm getting older, and my body parts, including my knees, were screaming, *"There is no way* you can live here the rest of your life." I bought my first house on that block in 1994. I love my neighborhood. John loved it, too. We knew and loved all the neighbors. The neighbors loved us.

Across the street from my stately Victorian was a one-story, mid-century-modern commercial building that was being rented and used as an adult day care center. It was an oddity in the turn-of-the-twentieth century neighborhood. The building had seen better days. It was horrendously ugly. Maintenance had been ignored. The roof leaked. The owners of the day-care business had had enough of the constant flow of leaking rainwater and one day packed up and moved. I contacted the owner and found out he was open to selling the building. That evening, John and I went for a walk. I steered him across the street and casually mentioned the building was vacant. "What would you think about doing a project like this?" I asked. In most expected fashion he said, "Absolutely not. Why on earth would we get involved in this?" I mentioned that as we got older, we might need a one-story home. I mentioned it could be a great investment. Then I said, "And look, we could build a roof-top deck." That inked the deal. After some intentional overselling on my part and engaging him in some interesting design options, John began to envision and create. He was open to a new project. And he was open to moving in together.

We bought the building. It was cheap, because we essentially purchased three walls and a deteriorated roof. The back wall was failing and had to be demolished and rebuilt. Due to the building's condition, there was nothing to salvage. We created a loft-style space from a three-quarter shell of a structure. Since we were starting from scratch, we designed the space intentionally so, as we got older, we could both age in place there. After eighteen months, both inside and out, the ugly was gone. There are no steps leading to the front door. The entrance is at grade with the sidewalk. We installed a walk-in, no-threshold shower. The house has wide doors. We weren't engaged in foreshadowing. How could we have known? Was it fate? Was it dumb luck? Were we guided? I don't know. I don't really believe in that. That supposes that John was more deserving than someone else. It supposes he was deserving of a place to comfortably die. I don't necessarily think "the good Lord was watching over us," as my mother, Mary, would often say. I think we just hit the lottery, as some people do. But ultimately, we lost the same lottery. We didn't get to age in place together. John just got to die in place.

Numbness and Tingling

The plan to combine households began in spring of 2019. By fall, the purchase was complete and work had begun. Construction progressed through the winter. Then, in March 2020, the Covid bomb exploded into the world, upending everyone's life. We didn't know it at the time, but there was another bomb ticking. Throughout 2021, John started experiencing numbness and tingling in his right arm and hand. It began gradually, but numbing increased with time. Our bodies change as we get older, but this was not normal. John first went to his primary-care physician, who referred him to a neurologist. We all know you can't just get a quick doctor's appointment. In our health-care culture, time is not on our side. Time was not on John's side. The next year and a half were a series of appointments and nerve conduction tests. The tests would return inconclusive, so he'd go back for more. One crackpot doctor pronounced him to have carpal tunnel syndrome and wanted to do surgery. John always followed the rules. If a doctor said, "Go," he'd go. To this day, I'm not sure why John didn't agree to surgery, but he didn't. As the numbness and tingling got worse, he then began to lose functionality and mobility. The arm became more and more useless. Pain and discomfort increased. The pain originally started as aching. As time went on John's arm started throbbing. It then increased to shooting pains down into his hand. Nights proved difficult. Many nights he would go to bed before getting up to move to the sofa. He thought sitting upright eased the pain a bit. This was brutality at its worst, for both of us. Finally, after a year of decline, his neurologist ordered an MRI.

A full year before John's diagnosis, the new house wasn't completely finished, but it was getting close. We didn't live there yet. The kitchen was substantially done. The bathrooms were functional. John and I were really excited about the new house. We were in the throes of Covid. Social gatherings were very discouraged. John said, "Screw it. Let's invite people over for an illegal Thanksgiving dinner." One brother was in town for the holiday, and his other brother was scheduled to be out of town. It would be a small Thanksgiving gathering for eight with the two of us, John's son, and John's brother and his family. But when the world is in Covid lockdown, a dinner party for eight is like a party for 50. We instructed people to keep those phones in their pockets. No photos allowed. None of us wanted to get yelled at. Yes, it was a gathering we probably shouldn't have hosted, but John was excited about our new house. John's dad had died earlier in March, and John wanted to be with his family. We didn't know it at the time, but John would only have a few years left to live himself. He was always close to his family, but that Thanksgiving began for him what became four years of intimacy and togetherness that is irreplaceable.

A year passed. In late November 2021, John had his MRI scheduled. Throughout the year, he still had some use in his right hand, but it had gotten progressively worse. We didn't know why John's arm and hand were becoming nonfunctioning. John wanted to have his family over again for Thanksgiving, Act II. It was the same cast of characters. One brother was in town. One brother was out of town. Right before this Thanksgiving, his condition had really worsened, and he wasn't able to use his right hand or arm at all. We always called John a "hippie." Nothing ever fazed him. He didn't get in a hurry. If that train was barreling toward him, he'd saunter out of the way and somehow not get hit. In our life together, that personality trait was my biggest thorn. But it was who he was, and that worked for him. I suggested he should "come out" with his condition to the family when they came over for Thanksgiving dinner. John wasn't so sure. His position was that he didn't want to tell anyone and alarm them if he didn't yet know what was wrong. His decline had started in the Covid year when we were rarely seeing people. His family knew there were issues, but they didn't know the extent of his mobility problem.

As we were setting the table before anyone arrived, I said, "John, you have to tell them. They are going to notice that I'm getting your plate for you and cutting your turkey." He agreed. He told them. But he emphasized there wasn't anything to worry about. He had an "MRI scheduled, but it was probably just carpal tunnel." John's family was close. They saw each other often. We all pitched in with everyone's projects, so they knew something was wrong. But after he mentioned his upcoming test, no one seemed particularly shaken by the escalation. They were just relieved he had a test scheduled and could proceed with a treatment plan. After all, John wasn't worried. And neither were they.

Dreams

Oh, the dreams.

Soon after John died, friends and family started asking me if I had had any "visits." Maybe. I don't know if I believe in that. Maybe I believe. Maybe I don't. I had some odd things occur. Are they weird? Sure. Are they unusual? Sure. Are they John coming back to visit me? I don't know.

I see him in my dreams often. I'm not sure if it's once a week or twice a week because I don't always remember my dreams. Some weeks I think it's more than once or twice. But oftentimes, I will wake up and know he was there but cannot recall what the dream was. Sometimes I'll remember it, but it might be nonsensical. The dreams aren't always pleasant. They sometimes make me sad or make me realize how much I miss John. Or sometimes they are just really uncomfortable. I once had a dream that we were on vacation together and sleeping in the same bed. John woke me up really angry and told me to get away from him. He told me he didn't want me touching him. In the dream, I was calm and knew he wasn't angry at me. I knew the source of the anger was his cancer. I never once saw John lash out in anger over his cancer. When I woke, I wondered if John's anger in the dream was really my anger at his cancer. Or maybe that night he was angry in the afterlife. When friends want a John dream, they don't realize it could be a horribly upsetting dream. But there are the good ones. Recently, I dreamt I was sleeping, and John came over and lay with me and held me. I'm lucky to still see him often. But I don't really think it's him in his spiritual form. I'm doubtful it is a visit from him. I think it's me holding on to him, trying not to forget. A couple of months after John died, I was questioning everything that happened and how I could have made it better. One night, when I dreamt we were together, he turned to me, and said, "Don't cry. Just be grateful for what we had."

I've experienced strange occurrences since John passed away. I tend to live my life in the practical realm. Don't get me wrong. I don't not believe. I have no idea what happens when we die. I would like to think that our life's energy (our essence, our soul) doesn't evaporate. And science tells us that energy doesn't dissipate. It changes form. But what does that mean as our flesh ceases to live? I have no idea. Anyone who tells you they know for sure is either a narcissist or a liar looking to get into your wallet. We won't know until it's over for us. And maybe then we won't know. Maybe it's black. Maybe it's daisies and angels. Maybe it's hot and agony. No one knows this secret.

A week after John left, I was understandably in a fog. I'm not a technology guy, but I can get by. I'm pushing 60 years old. I use a computer for work. I use my phone to make calls, send texts, check email, take a pic that probably won't ever be seen again, and play Wordle. It had only been a week since John had passed away, and I was tinkering in the garage. I have no idea what I was doing out there. It was probably something frivolous that seemed really important. Maybe I was organizing the wrenches when I faintly heard some music. We always had music playing wherever we were. We rarely had the TV on. I heard some generic instrumental tune that I wouldn't have on a playlist. I didn't have a speaker in the garage, so I was a bit confused. I realized it was coming from my phone in my pocket. Full disclosure: shit happens inadvertently on that phone in my pocket a lot. I recently "pocket" texted gibberish to a friend, causing her to reply, "Are you having a stroke?" I pulled the phone out to see a collage of photos playing, and the folder was titled "The Group's All Here Apr 21, 2018–Sep 18, 2024." It was a slideshow of pictures of John and me with that ridiculous song playing. I was completely freaked out. I didn't want to touch the screen because I didn't know where it came from. I had never seen a slideshow like that. If I stopped it, I didn't know if it would ever come back. I didn't know where to find it. I've since learned that in my Samsung photo gallery there is a tab called "Stories." I've had a Samsung for years. I had never seen it. I had never opened it. But that day it opened in my pocket, on its own. My reasonable self says that wasn't John, but I still cried.

We were a music household. John *loved* singer-songwriter Neko Case. We saw her in concert many times. And when he was really sick and in bed, he would tell Alexa to play music by Neko. When his brother, Kevin, would stay with him, I'd get home and Kevin would say, "Yeah, he was in bed all day, but he had me play that Neko Case, whoever that is." One of Neko's more well-known songs is "I Wish I Was the Moon." According to her recent memoir, she wrote that song as her father's health was in a state of decline. John loved the song, along with much of her catalog. The album on which that song was included was released in 2002. A month and a day after John left, I woke up one morning and saw the moon out of the top of my window. I have shades that cover the bottom, but the top quarter of the window is exposed to let the light in at daybreak. I woke up before 6:00 a.m. on November 15 to see an amazing supermoon. Still lying in bed, I said out loud to no one, "Goddammit, John. 'I wish I was the moon tonight.'"

I got up. I grabbed a cup of coffee. I brought my coffee in the shower and turned on the water. The walk-in shower features a shelf for your coffee or a cocktail (if you've been working all day). I turned on a satellite radio station. A few songs played. I let the hot water flow over me to waken me for work. Out of the speaker came a few simple guitar chords. Then I heard the word "chimney," followed by the word "falls." And Neko began belting out "I Wish I Was the Moon" on the radio. I've never heard that song on satellite radio. I've never heard that song played anywhere except on my playlist or at one of her shows. The song came out twenty-two years earlier in 2002. Was it random? I don't know. Was it John? I don't know. I had a brief thought that maybe John hadn't completely left me yet. Oddly enough, I didn't have a meltdown. I didn't cry. I just thought, *Oh, isn't that sweet?*

Potato Salad

John was absolutely a self-identified food snob. He wasn't exactly prissy about food, but if you were going to contribute something to the table, you damn sure better bring your "A" game. John was a rule follower. John was a great cook because, by golly, he followed that recipe like it was the Ten Commandments. Me? Not so much. Lots of times I take liberties. Or I might just make it up. John loved my potato salad. I make it the way my mother, Mary, makes it: potatoes, hard boiled eggs, dill pickles, celery, mayo, salt, and pepper. No measurements needed. You just put in however much you put in. And it's damn good. While I improvise, I sometimes come across recipes I want to try. Maybe they work. Maybe they don't. Maybe they need a little spicing up. Years ago, I found a recipe for three-pepper barbecued potato salad that looked interesting. Red and yellow bell peppers were mixed with new potatoes and tossed with a dressing of barbecue sauce for a colorful starchy summer treat. I mentioned to John we were having potato salad, and he eagerly awaited dinnertime. He took one bite of my new recipe and was pissed. I think the exact phrasing went, "You make the best potato salad in the world. Why on earth would you make this? You can just throw that recipe in the trash." I didn't think it was terrible, but for John, it was a huge missed opportunity for a potato salad he loved. We laughed for years about the barbecued potato salad failure. From then on, every time I made potato salad, he'd raise those eyebrows with a look that dared me to do it again.

The River House

John, right, and me in Chester, Illinois, before cancer, spring 2019

In 2004, John and I bought a cheap, dilapidated, 1,100-square-foot folk Victorian house on the Mississippi River bluffs. It gave us a place to go. It gave us something to do. It gave us a place to rest. It gave us a place to recover. It gave us a place to just be. Vivid memories are with me always, but they are particularly poignant at the river.

Located in Chester, Illinois, the house stands a story and a half with wood lap siding. It sits on the bluff and has a magnificent view of the Mississippi River and Missouri farmland. The high view looks down perfectly over the river, the watery line between Illinois and Missouri. Each season brings a different and stunning portrait of Midwest farm fields and life on the Mississippi River as you gaze over the horizon. Winter features ice chunks floating down the river and a white blanket as far as the eye can see. In the summer, deer graze

The River House in Chester

on the river bottoms, and buzzards circle, searching for dinner. In the fall, shades of orange and yellow drape from the live oaks and frame a portrait of the river. Spring brings cool, crisp, glistening frost as the world begins to be reborn. And American Bald Eagles that make their homes on the banks of the river glide through the air with their immense wings spread wide.

In the early 2000s, living in St. Louis, I had a neighbor who retired and was looking for a retirement home town. She had family that was born in Chester, Illinois, and found an 1830s stone house overlooking the Mississippi as her retirement home. Chester sits 60 miles south of St. Louis as the crow flies. In May, 2004, she called me and said there was a house next door to her with a river view that had just gone into foreclosure. I had visited her several times as she was rehabbing her house, and she suggested John and I come down to take a look at the newly vacant home. I curtly said, "There are lots of things I need in this world, and a house in Chester isn't one of them. Especially in Chester." I had nothing against Chester, but it was an hour-and-a-half drive. It just didn't seem practical. My friend sent photos and told me the house had a "million-dollar view." That was clearly a bit of puffery designed to entice me to take the bait. I later found out she was worried the house would be purchased as a low-end rental. She sent me the listing, and I thought, *Holy cow. You can't buy a car for that price.* I was intrigued.

John and I took a late Saturday afternoon drive down to see the house we were certainly not going to buy. The great thing about the Midwest is that it's sweltering in the summer, and it's frigid in the winter. It's the best of those two worlds. That also means houses can be affordable. The day we closed, we walked in to find a dead raccoon in the utility room. Several weeks afterward, we found a dead groundhog stuck in the wall. We bought a complete gut job that had been badly "modernized" over the years and smelled like animal piss. The first year, we pitched a tent and camped in the yard until we could get the piss and dead-animal smell out of the house. When John and I were pulling out the crumbling plaster one of the first weekends we were there, John looked over at me and said, "I see people doing this on TV. I *never* thought those people would be me." Twenty-one years after John and I bought the house we swore we weren't going to buy, it's still not completely "finished." But projects are about the process. And sometimes projects can be about just being together.

Each weekend the house got a little better and a little more livable. We replaced systems. We finished rooms. We painted. We started sleeping inside. We made that crappy little house a weekend home, and we made a life of fun. The view offers a stunning snapshot of God's Midwest creation. Nothing compares to sitting on the porch as the dawn fades or the sunset appears. The sky fills with colors of red and pink and blue and lilac and fuchsia. As the sky disappears to darkness and the stars brighten, it's a wondrous spectacle. And that's why we bought a weekend house in Chester.

For many years, John and I talked about tearing off the old dilapidated side and back porches and building replacements. The dream was to make a wraparound porch that spanned from the western-facing river side around to the southern-facing back of the house. The back side has a view of the river as well. A second-story deck on the western side to be accessed from a dormer in roofline was a must. But there was always a more important project like new wiring or a kitchen and bathroom remodel. We did a lot of the alterations ourselves over the years. A two-story porch and deck, however, were a bit ambitious. That was a project we needed to hire out. Also, our lives had taken a bit of a chaotic turn with John's health issues. About a year after John was diagnosed with cancer, we finally contracted someone to build the dream porch we had talked about for eighteen years. And as all construction projects seem to go, this one stretched on and on. One day John said, "Just tell him I really want to be able to sit on this porch before I die." John enjoyed that porch for eleven months.

John always loved the weekends at the river. Last summer, when John's health was getting worse by the day, we still came to the river house. I'd cut the grass. He couldn't do much of anything. But he'd sit out on our dream porch and watch me work in the yard. He so much wanted to contribute. He so much wanted to help me. He'd always tell me how good the yard looked. Maybe it did. Maybe it didn't. Maybe he couldn't tell if it looked good or not. His contribution was to support me. So now, when I'm in Chester cutting the grass, I'm sweaty, my heart pumps, and I'm alone with myself on the green terrain and the small hills. I see a vision of John sitting up on that porch watching me work in the yard, and I see him watching the barges go by.

Christmas in a Hospital Room

The week after Thanksgiving in 2021, John had the first of what would turn out to be very many MRIs. After the inaugural test was completed, the radiologist told John he could see the problem. He saw a growth on his neck he believed to be a nerve sheath tumor. The radiologist explained this to be a growth that develops within the protective sheath surrounding the nerves. He indicated most of these tumors are benign. John was then referred to a neurological surgeon whose first available appointment was *in late February*, almost three months later. This appointment was not to schedule surgery. This was only a consultation. Nothing was available before then. John would have to continue to sleep sitting up, writhing with pain shooting down his arm for another three months until he could get a consultation. Because John was a rule follower, if that was when he could get in, that was going to have to be good enough. On the other hand, I couldn't sit back and do nothing. I started calling everyone I knew to try to find someone else to see him. I'm not connected to the medical field, but there had to be someone we knew that could get him in sooner. I even contacted someone in Atlanta who had St. Louis connections. It turned out that we wouldn't need a connection. The earthquake was starting its rumble.

A good friend, Sue, was at the river house with us a couple of weeks after John's MRI. It was a week before Christmas. That weekend, John started having pain and numbness in his abdomen, a new development. As Sue tells it, we were having dinner Saturday night when John excused himself from the table. She looked over to see John was gray. She said

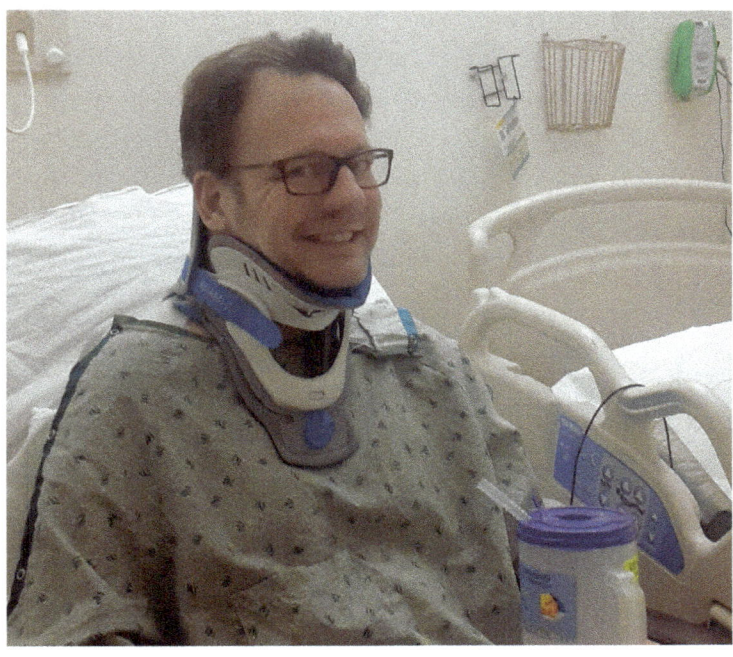

John, after surgery to remove the mass growing on his spine, January 2022

he looked like he was in complete misery. In fine John fashion, in a few minutes he recovered, and we went on with the evening. Sue later told me that she felt like she overstepped when she said to me as she was leaving the next day, "I'd put him in the car and get him to the ER immediately." I don't remember her telling me that. But I do remember thinking we had to somehow escalate getting him care.

We returned to St. Louis the next afternoon on a Sunday. I have another really good friend, Ana, who is a nurse. Not only is she a nurse, she's reasonable and practical and gets things done. Ana adopts and takes care of the entire universe: humans and animals alike. She's like St. Francis. Especially in the last year, we relied on Ana for a multitude of tasks and advice surrounding John's predicament. She knows how to work the system. Since John's MRI showed a growth, she also had been brainstorming ideas and solutions to get John some more immediate care since he couldn't get into a neurologist until February. We called Ana on the way back to St. Louis and asked her to come over and help us formulate a plan. That evening, we sat down and pulled together a timeline of his issues and a synopsis of what care and tests he had already received. She suggested that, the next morning, he go to the preeminent hospital system in St. Louis that specializes in cancer care. She said while nerve sheath tumors were often benign, it would be wise to go to the best system for cancer care. Ana helped us get into his MyChart to allow permissions for the records to be shared with other providers. We packed a bag.

I thought we should take John to the hospital that Sunday evening. Ana convinced me otherwise. She explained that hospitals are busy on the weekends due to accidents and shootings. And, apparently, Sundays are a popular ER day because people show up for care if they need a doctor's note explaining their Monday work absence. Ana thought we both needed a good night's sleep, and we probably wouldn't be seen any quicker if we arrived the night before. Okay. I never really thought that through. On Monday morning, December 20, we arrived at the Barnes Jewish Medical Center Emergency Room in St. Louis. We waited all day. Then we waited some more. Nurses came in. They documented charts. Doctors came in and poked John with little needles to determine his ability to feel the instrument (none). Occupational therapists came in and asked him to squeeze a ball. Nope. Residents came in and reviewed his medical history. Finally, after enduring the Emergency Room circus for nearly 16 hours, John was admitted to the Neurology ward.

The days in the neuro ward may have been some of the craziest I've experienced. Mentally, John was fine. He just had a tumor on his neck. And because John was mentally stable and healthy, he quickly became the favorite patient on the neuro floor. Patients scream. They hit the nurses. Some have to be restrained. Alarms go off. It seemed every hour there was a loud commotion or emergency somewhere on that floor. Those nurses and staff wear both scrubs and halos to work. John had a roommate separated by a curtain. His first roommate was pretty ordinary. He wasn't a screamer. He wasn't violent. He was an older gentleman in his seventies, and he had his wife with him. Based on appearances, which don't always prove to be true, I think he could have been from a rural part of the region. People come from all over to this hospital. It's possible John's roommate didn't know any gay couples, or at least, he maybe hadn't been exposed to different groups of people. The flimsy curtain between the beds was hardly a barrier separating patients' lives. Even though discretion was encouraged, everything was seen and heard. Patients, families, doctors, nurses, and staff incessantly came and went from the room. One night, after John got wheeled away for a test, John's roommate passed me going to the restroom and said, "Are you John's father?" *What the actual fuck,* I thought. John was fifty-seven years old and I was fifty-five. I was under just a little pressure, and I reflexively blurted out, "No. But I sure am his Daddy." I thought the nurse was going to hit the floor. Her eyes got enormous, her mouth gaped open, and her face said, "OMG." She put her hand over her mouth, muffled a laugh, and ran from the room. The roommate didn't talk to us again.

That Tuesday and Wednesday consisted of a series of doctors, tests, scans, and MRIs. Covid was still rampant. The vaccine had been approved by the FDA and released a few weeks prior to John being admitted to the hospital, but the shot wasn't yet being widely distributed. Patients were scared. Visitors were scared. Nurses were scared. We were scared. Of Covid. And of a tumor. But at least John was finally getting treated and finally getting care. The hospital scheduled surgery to remove the growth on his neck on December 23.

The two days prior to surgery also gave us the opportunity to get word to John's son, his two brothers, and our family and friends. Those two days were excruciating. John wasn't a worrier. But this weighed heavily. The surgeon would operate on his spinal column around nerves that controlled body function. And the surgical area was immediately adjacent to the brain.

Thursday morning John went into surgery to remove what was thought to be a nerve sheath tumor. John's brother, Kevin, came to the hospital and waited with me. I think surgery took about six hours, but that timeline is blurry. After what seemed like an eternity,

I got the call from the surgeon. He said, "John is out of surgery and in recovery. He did fine. His growth was not attached to the nerve sheath. It was attached to his spinal column. We couldn't remove all of the tumor due to its placement on the spine because we didn't want to risk further paralysis. I hate to be the one to tell you this, but his growth is cancerous and malignant. We won't know for sure what it is until his biopsy results come back."

Constant Tunes

Music was always playing in our house. Music still plays in my house. There is much more audio than video in my space. John and I would attend live music as much as possible. The summer after John had surgery to remove the tumor, Natalie Merchant came to town. He really wanted to see her. We remembered Natalie Merchant as the cool indie rocker from the band 10,000 Maniacs in the eighties. We remembered ourselves as the young, cool, indie rock fans. Sometimes we don't realize what age does to us and those around us. John used a cane that night. He was weak and wobbly. I needed knee replacements and hobbled around. At that show we realized we were no longer in our twenties. Natalie was no longer in her twenties. Those around us were no longer in their twenties. The median age of the crowd was probably sixty-five. I spied no fewer than three walkers and two people on oxygen. Never one to lose his sense of humor, John turned to me and remarked, "Compared to these people, we could be on the damn Olympic track and field team." Somehow, we all got old in the last thirty-five years.

Even as John's health declined the summer before his death, he still wanted to go to shows. There were times that he just didn't feel well enough to make a concert. But I would always get him a ticket, and it would often be a game-day decision if he felt up to going. Most times, if he wasn't up for it, I would still go, and I had friends on standby who would use the ticket. Toward the end, friends would be on standby to stay with John if I still wanted to attend a show. During his health journey, he prioritized seeing live music because he

John with our friend, Ana, at a music festival, September 2017

knew he was running out of time. And he saw some of his favorite musicians. He went to Nashville to see the Floating Men. We saw Allison Russell and Kyshona Armstrong. We sailed for a week on a music cruise. He made it to a Kelly Willis show. He saw Shovels and Rope. After he missed the Sierra Ferrell concert because of chemo, she came around again, and he made that show. In 2023, we traveled to Chicago to see Neko Case and Guster. After we bought tickets for the Chicago trip, he said, "I really want to see Neko one more time before I die." Check. He did. But then he would say it again and again and again. If John had lived to be 100, he would have said he wanted to see Neko one more time before he died.

By the summer of 2024, John had lost the use of both arms and hands, but he was still walking okay. Sometimes, he'd be a little unstable, and we'd hold onto him. He could usually maneuver himself fairly well. The hand paralysis was a challenge if he had to go to a public restroom. He couldn't get his pants up or down. I could go in and help, but bigger crowded venues were always a concern. He consciously limited his cocktails (and other liquids) on show days so he wouldn't inconveniently need to go to the restroom. In June of that year, Jon Batiste came to town. John had never seen him, and he was really looking forward to that concert. Getting him to that show remains one of my fondest memories. The show had lots of energy and was really uplifting. I had attended a couple of Jon Batiste shows and knew that the encore would be a conga line weaving through the seats and the crowd. We stayed for just enough of the conga line to see it, but we really needed to get John out before it got too chaotic. He was thrilled with the show. It was the highlight of his summer.

Ana, right, and me in Miami before a vacation music cruise, February 2024 (Photo by John)

Six weeks before John passed away, some friends and I got him to a Charley Crockett concert. He was in a rapid decline at that point, and it was pretty difficult on John. During the show, his brother gave him a shot of Morphine. He could no longer use his hands, so we smuggled in a straw so he could drink bourbon as we held his drink. It was pretty difficult to watch. But Neko Case was coming to town again in September. Once again, John said, "I really want to make it to one more Neko show." Neko showed up five days too late.

Caregiver Training

After John lost the use of his right arm and hand, he was always worried about losing more and more extremity function. He was extremely worried about losing his left arm and legs. And that eventually did happen. Part of the fear around his function loss was how he could continue to live in our home. Would he need to go to a skilled nursing facility? He wanted to stay in his home, but he didn't want to burden me. Like many others who face the same predicament, I maintained that he would always live in our home. I was trained for this.

I don't know why the same life themes show up over and over. I grew up around illness and infirmity. When I was eleven, my family moved into a house my parents built on the "compound." My paternal grandparents lived next door to the right. My aunt and uncle lived next door to the left. This made unauthorized high school parties inconvenient, but not impossible. I just made everyone pile into one or two cars and stay in the house.

Shortly after we moved in, my aunt was diagnosed with cancer. She went through chemotherapy, and it seemed she was sick all the time. I would go sit with her and sometimes clean up when she would vomit. She didn't win the battle with her disease. On the other side of the house, my grandmother was ill. I don't really remember when it started, but she developed Alzheimer's and dementia shortly after we moved in. It got bad fairly quickly. She stopped walking early in her diagnosis because she was afraid. I suppose she was afraid of falling. But she had wandered off from the property a time or two and walked down the road. Maybe she was also afraid of getting lost.

There was never a question about her going to a nursing home. It wouldn't happen, and it wasn't even discussed. Maybe nursing homes weren't as prevalent back then. Maybe they were, but our family didn't have the resources for that. Most likely, there was just an understandable determination that she wasn't going to live somewhere other than her home. I think probably there wasn't even a decision to be made. Our family went there daily and brought or cooked dinner that we all ate together. Eventually, as her condition worsened, we started spoon feeding her. In the mornings before work or school, we would go next door and get her out of bed. We would stand her up, get her in a wheelchair, and move her from room to room. Gradually, she became nonverbal but would respond with a head nod, a head shake, or a smile. Eventually, that stopped, too. No one knew if she heard us, saw us, or knew we had put her in her chair in the den to watch her soap opera "stories." In the evenings, we would put her back in bed.

That was in the 1980s. At some point, someone in the family procured a rolling contraption that looked like a hammock attached to a big arm. The fabric mesh hammock clipped onto a long steel arm that arched overhead. We called it the Sling. The arm was head high, and if you weren't paying attention, it was the source of a nice bump on the forehead. The arm and vertical pole fit into a rolling stand that was shaped like a "V." When Granny was in bed, we would roll her onto her side, put the fabric hammock on the bed, scoot it under her as best we could, then roll her the other way and straighten out the fabric. The fabric needed to be as straight as possible so as not to create sores. We lowered the arm by a crank, hooked the hammock onto the arm, and cranked it up until she was off the bed. Then we'd roll the contraption into the den, plop her in the chair, and turn on those stories. Miraculously, I don't ever remember her ending up on the floor. I always wondered if she thought she was on a ride at Six Flags.

The caretaking lasted eleven years, nine of which she was bedridden. It seems horrible. And it was horrible. But there were plenty of laughs. The more serious the situation when laughing was prohibited, the more hilarious the events became. The caregiving started when I was a preteen when old people were alien beings and bodily functions were sidesplitting. Catheter bags, food, smells, and interaction with an assortment of personalities coming in and out of the house was a constant source of entertainment and laughter. It was a difficult period for everyone involved. But there was also a tremendous commitment and an incredible amount of love in that house. My mother, Mary, was the foreman even though she was "just" the daughter-in-law. But she loved my father and would do anything for him. He loved his parents, and she loved his parents, too. Even though I was too young to understand, it was an unbelievable training ground that taught me so much about life and love and death. It taught me about dignity and compassion. I learned an amazing amount about discipline. I learned perspective about what's truly important. I learned calmness in the midst of chaos. I learned to laugh in the midst of heartbreak.

Exhausted and Defeated

John knew that story. But I'm not sure he really understood what we did at my grandparents' house. I'm not sure anyone really can unless they lived it. John was worried about how he would spend his last days. I was confident, like many people, that he would spend that time at home. I was trained.

Even though I was trained, caring for John is the hardest thing I've ever done. John was an easy patient. He was so sweet and so kind and so compliant and so appreciative. He never went to a nursing facility, and I am thankful for the power team we had. I'm grateful for the tenacious attitudes we all (including John) possessed.

We both still worked. Even though John initially lost the use of his right hand, he continued to work as a customer service representative for the IRS. He had started working remotely during Covid. By the time Covid waned, John was approved to continue to work remotely under the Family and Medical Leave Act (FMLA). Even though he couldn't use his right hand, he could still use his left. He operated his computer, mouse, and phone system with his functioning hand.

My employer was amazing, too. I was approved to work remotely and could make up time as I was taking John to and from treatments and appointments. I went to all of John's appointments with him at the beginning. He needed to get his sea legs, both literally and figuratively, and get used to new routines. As he and I both got comfortable with the process and after he recovered from surgery and became stronger, he started driving himself to chemo and his appointments. He had an automatic transmission vehicle and could shift the car into gear and steer with his left hand. With a few exceptions due to a conflict, I always went to appointments when he saw his oncologist. Those first couple of years became pretty routine and fairly ordinary. Sure, it was a difficult juggle. There were a lot of things to keep up with, and it was hard emotionally. But we kept all the balls in the air those first couple of years.

It's hard to even explain the last six months of John's life. The locomotive was careening down the hill at full speed. There was no stopping it. I was trained as much as anyone could be, but how do you make it okay? It seemed every day brought a different problem. Every day brought new issues. Every day was a lesson in aborting the day's plan and doing something unexpected. But every day I committed myself to doing my best. I wouldn't dwell on what I did or didn't do well the day before. I had to bring my "A" game that day. I made a commitment each day to create a peaceful, loving, and calm environment in that home. I couldn't afford to let the little things derail the train. I couldn't afford to let the big things derail the train, either. Even when things went wrong, I looked every day into the face of someone I dearly loved who was dying before my eyes. The spilled coffee was hardly a problem. The car that wouldn't start was hardly a problem. Not making it to the bathroom on time was hardly a problem.

Some would say I should have been praying. It's not that I don't believe in the power of prayer, I just believe that God knows what we need. Things happen the way they are intended to happen. Instead of praying, every morning I would get up and say, "fuck". And every night I would go to bed and say, "fuck". Note the lack of punctuation in that one-word sentence. Note the lack of capitalization. There was no exclamation point. There was no question mark. There wasn't really even a period. I wasn't angry. I was just terribly sad. I was just terribly exhausted. I was just terribly defeated. And I didn't want John to know I was sad and exhausted and defeated. That wouldn't help the situation in the least.

The John Club

A new friend who didn't know John recently said to me, "Do you mind if I ask you 'X' about John?" I don't remember what the question was. I didn't mind at all her asking. I like when people ask. John's being is still alive in me. I don't want to lose that. Oddly for me, it seems new relationships are easier for me to navigate than some of the old relationships.

There is a core group of people who showed up for John. And they showed up for me. They heard it all. They saw it all. They felt it all. They watched him cry in pain. John watched them cry with him. They fed him. They sat with him. They got him pills. They took him to chemo. They had a drink with him. They gave him a Morphine shot. There is now a John Club. The John Club knows. There is comfort and power for me knowing they know. I will be forever bonded and tied to those people. Many people form significant and memorable bonds with those they met in high school. There are class reunions to reminisce about the "good old days." Those four short high-school years are formative at a time when children are growing into adulthood. For me, these last years with John were just as influential. I wonder if I will have an impenetrable bond with those who gave of themselves and were truly present during John's health journey. I think so. But maybe we'll move on and away from each other. Still, currently, those are the people I'm most comfortable around. They know the story. They walked with John and me during the story. They are part of the story. They are the John Club.

Then there are people who are friends, but they didn't see the horror of it all. They would occasionally come by or call. They may have dropped something off. They really don't know what happened in the days and hours before we opened the door and the days and hours after they left. Those are people I have a difficult time connecting or reconnecting with. I just find it hard to fill in the blanks. They know some things. Maybe they know some of the hard things. But I don't know how to tell them the rest of the story. Maybe they don't want to know. But this story is such an integral part of me that I can't separate myself from it.

People say that I'll forget the difficult times that I had with John. I'm not sure I believe that. I don't want to forget the difficult times. It was an honor and a privilege to be with him as he transitioned from this life. He left me with such a gift, and it is a blessing for which I'm incredibly grateful. For people who knew John but weren't in the trenches, those gifts and blessings are almost unexplainable.

So how is it easier with new friends? I get to tell the story as they want to know it. It may be difficult for them to hear, but it's not painful for them like it might be painful for those who knew John. And of course, I do want people to ask me who John was. I want people to ask me who John was for me. I want people to ask me what he was like. I want people to ask me about his life. There is a misconception that you shouldn't bring "it" up. I wonder if people think I'm going to cry, and it would be uncomfortable. I might cry. I very seriously doubt it. But if I were to cry, the source of those tears is certainly not the person asking me a question about John. My relationship with John is ingrained in me and is now part of my being. It's not an upsetting topic. While I wish John's end-of-life journey were different, it's part of our story that I want to share.

The Dead Spouse Club

My sister recently came to town for a visit. We have different personalities. I'm my mother's child. My sister is my father's child. But while we are very different, she's easy to be around. We love each other. She brought a college friend with her. Her college friend lost her husband from a heart attack twelve years ago. We're both in the "club." The Dead Spouse Club doesn't solicit applications. It's the club in which your membership is ordered, forced, and predetermined. The easy part with my sister's friend is there is no pretense, no bullshit. She knows. I know. No situation is exactly the same. But there are enough common threads and common experiences to be relatable.

I've found weekends with people particularly difficult. That weekend was palatable because I've got an easy sibling, and her friend and I are in the same club. However, typically, long periods of time with people are taxing. I can easily pull it together, relate, and be present for a couple of hours. Longer periods take a lot more energy. John and I were together 21 years. We were an extension of one another. When we would host people for a weekend, or even a long evening, we could tag-team the guests. I would cook, and he would chat with them before I would come into the gathering for a bit. Then, we'd sit down for a meal. He might clean up while I had a drink with the guests. We had entertaining and being with people down to a science. Now, I'm the only host to those guests.

In John's sick years, our togetherness was a constant. That constant togetherness formed a tight bond of amazing intimacy, even when it was unspoken. Since John died, when I've been around people for an extended time, it feels artificial to me. It almost feels like a show. Even worse, sometimes it feels like an audition for a show. The "audition" is me trying to convince others that I'm okay. And I am okay. But people have that question.

The creation of new relationships and intimacy doesn't yet have the same draw. In a way, I don't want it. People ask me if I'm lonely. I don't know. Maybe sometimes. But I don't want a new partner. I don't want new intimacy. I don't want a new life. I want my old partner. I want the old intimacy. I want my old life.

I don't think that means I'm stuck. I'm not devastated. I'm functional. I'm as happy as can be expected. I've known people to marry immediately after a spouse dies. Everyone has different needs. That's just not presently a need for me. In hindsight, I used to say something horrifying to John before he got sick. I would say, "If you ever leave me or die, I'm not doing this again. I'm not training another one." He'd laugh and say, "You'll find one that's already trained." I can't imagine partnering again. I'm not opposed to it. I just can't imagine it.

The Secret

John was so completely easy to love. He was kind. He was funny. He was cute. He was dedicated. He was never annoyed. He was tall. He had beautiful blue eyes. He had a great laugh. He loved seeing people, being with people. Even on his worst days, he was never angry. Even when he didn't feel good, he was a good host. He was an easy cancer patient.

When John was diagnosed, we tried to go about our daily lives as normally as possible. We had an active social life and social circle. As the cancer got worse and John deteriorated, we made the decision to keep seeing people. He wanted it. I wanted it for him. So, there were always people in and out of the house. His family came over. Our friends and neighbors came over. I had lived on the block for almost 30 years. My old house and yard were the gathering places for our tight group of neighbor friends. The new house we constructed across the street from my old house logically became the new gathering place. Even after John got sick, he still wanted to see his people. When someone came over for a visit, John always kept it together. Some would say that he put on a brave face. Really, though, that face was authentic. He liked being around people. He wanted to have a good time. He wanted others to have a good time. When people showed up, his adrenaline would kick in, and he was completely in the moment. Granted, he would be exhausted by the time they left. And they didn't know he crashed minutes after they were gone.

About a month before John died, the neighbors called an impromptu happy hour on our back patio. It started with one or two people. Then, before long, it was a ten-person party. John was the ultimate host. Happy hour started around 5:00 p.m., and he hung tough for a couple of hours. John hadn't eaten dinner, and it was approaching 8:00 p.m. I told everyone we needed to go inside so John could eat. The patio has windows looking into the dining room. John was still walking, but not well. I helped him inside, and I spoon-fed him dinner. At the end of the meal, he said, "I just can't go back out there." I told him I would break up the party. He said, "No. Let them stay. They are having fun. But I really need to go to bed." But before he went to bed, he asked me to help him back to the patio door so he could thank everyone for coming and tell them to have a good evening. That was the last time they saw him.

I sometimes wonder if we didn't let people in on the real secret, the dying secret. We talked about it with people. Maybe our words didn't match what they were seeing. We both had an irreverent attitude toward the situation. John would explain that he couldn't use his right arm and hand because he "caught the cancer." People wouldn't know if they could laugh until he'd put on that Mona Lisa half-smile and cut his eyes over in a side glance. Maybe we made it seem better than it really was. Sure, our friends knew he was sick and on pain medication. When someone would ask me, "How's John?" the only answer I could give them was, "Well, you know he caught the cancer. And he still has it." I may have told them he had a good week, whatever that means. Unless you were around a lot, you wouldn't know. And when John died, our family and friends were *shocked*. That made no sense to me. They didn't know it was the end. Or maybe they just didn't want to know.

I've been to gatherings since John left. They're mostly pretty dreadful for me. It's human nature, I guess, but largely people don't know what to say to me. Usually, it's people I've known for a long time. Or they are people John knew for a long time. At first, I struggled with the uncomfortable space between us. I quickly made the conscious choice to let the tension be. It's not my job to put words in their mouths. I've been through some pretty heavy trauma in the past four years. An uncomfortable silence ranks very low on my problem list.

I have no idea how to answer the questions, "How are *you*?" or "How are you, *really*?" I'm pretty sure everyone knows the answer to those two questions. I'm also reluctant to truly answer those questions at a jolly happy hour. I respect those who come up to me and say, "I'm sure the adjustment is hard. How are things different for you?" "Is your relationship with John's family still, okay?" "What are the things you miss most about having John around?" "I know you cooked three meals a day. Are you eating fast food every meal now? Or are you drinking your way through meals?" Mostly, though, the words that ring the truest are, "I am really sorry. I know this is terrible. I wouldn't have wanted it for John, and I don't want this for you." That simple acknowledgment stretches so far. I've come to understand that I crave the acknowledgment that someone meaningful to me and to the world is no longer with us. As the world continues to move as if nothing happened, I don't want John's "body of work" to disappear.

John, left, with Liam, middle, and me celebrating Liam's 24th birthday, October 2021

Happy Birthday Tracy

In the early days of our relationship, I had a birthday party for John. It could have been for his fortieth. It seems like we would have had a gathering for that. Our friend, Ana, and I went to Sam's to get a cake. We perused the sheet cake section and found one with colors that we liked. The cake department had written messages on some of them to entice you to buy a cake with a personalized message. One of the cakes spelled out "Happy Birthday Tracy." I told Ana, "We have to buy that cake. Let's show up with a Happy Birthday Tracy cake just for fun." We did. John's son, Liam, was about seven at the time. He thought that was the funniest joke in the world. For a seven-year-old it was as funny as a fart. Random "Happy Birthday Tracy" cakes would appear at various parties for years.

We all celebrate important milestone dates: birthdays, anniversaries, engagements, graduations. This past year, John's birthday came and went. There wasn't a Tracy cake. I knew it was his sixty-first birthday. It didn't elicit much emotion. His death anniversary date came and went. Again, it was just another day. Those special days seem anticlimactic because John's fingerprints are everywhere around me. The "remembrance" days don't seem all that important because each day brings its own version of loss. The death anniversary wasn't any worse than every other day. In the future, as the rawness subsides, maybe the milestone dates will mean something more. Maybe I'll order a "Happy Birthday Tracy" cake.

Ewing Sarcoma

After his operation Christmas week of 2021, John's surgeon called me and told me his tumor was cancerous. John spent a few more weeks in the hospital. After all, he had surgery on his spinal column. The operation removed part of the growth located between his C5 and C6 discs. Doctors came in and out of his hospital room. They poked him with needles to gauge his sensory ability. They constantly checked his wound. They asked him simple questions hoping he could give simple answers. Physical therapists were in and out. They wanted him out of bed and walking. They tested his muscle strength and his range of motion ability. Occupational therapists were in and out. The occupational therapists would bring him a ball to squeeze. Or they would bring him some clay to mold. He couldn't do it. He couldn't move his hand at all. He could move his arm from the shoulder joint and elbow, but the hand was dead. I wondered if he just wasn't trying hard enough. Our friend told us about a video she had watched where a guy was paralyzed in one hand. He tied his functional hand behind his back until he regained use of the paralyzed hand. I thought maybe John could try that. That may have been just the first of the many foolish thoughts and ideas I would have over the next three years.

I don't remember exactly when the doctors told John and me the results of the biopsy. Frankly, there is a lot I don't remember. Sometimes, I feel like those three years were a big blur. Maybe it was in the hospital. Maybe it wasn't. I have no idea. Because John was admitted to the Emergency Room at Barnes Jewish Christian Hospital (BJC), he continued his care with that hospital group. The BJC system is affiliated with Washington University in St. Louis. The system has great doctors, incredible research teams, and first-rate facilities.

At some point after his surgery, someone relayed to him that his cancer was Ewing Sarcoma. Ewing Sarcoma is a rare cancer that affects bone and soft tissue. It is most common in children and young adults with most patients being diagnosed between 5–20 years old. John was 57 at the time of his diagnosis. We don't know why. We don't know how. The doctors don't know why or how. That's just the hand that he was dealt.

John didn't see an oncologist immediately after being discharged. I believe it was four to six weeks after surgery. He needed time to heal from the tumor removal operation. But I remember his first appointment with the oncologist who would become his lifeline for the next three years. At the first meeting with the cancer doctor, she explained that she was a specialist in sarcomas and only treated sarcoma patients. John liked her. That's all that mattered to me. She went on to say that she would meet with a team of doctors each week to review her patients' files. As a team, they would recommend a course of treatment and care. While John's surgery was considered successful, they were unable to remove all of the growth due to its location on the spine. His oncologist indicated that John's treatment protocol would be seventeen rounds of chemotherapy and thirty-three rounds of radiation. Halfway through the chemotherapy treatments, he would stop and undergo the thirty-three radiation treatments. If all was going well, he would then resume chemotherapy after radiation. If his body could endure the curative action, she estimated he would be in treatment for approximately sixteen months.

The most important thing she said that day was, "I don't see why we can't get this taken care of."

Marriage

John and I never married. We were together for twenty-one years. For the first twelve years, same-sex marriage wasn't legal. We first got together in our late thirties. We both grew up in the seventies and eighties when it wasn't even possible for two men or two women to get legally married. When that trend started changing, I think we both had a "meh" attitude about a wedding. I know many same-sex couples our age who wanted marriage, and thankfully they were able fulfill that dream for themselves. Many couples I know got married multiple times because state legislatures started legalizing same sex marriage, but it still wasn't a federal right.

For us, marriage just wasn't that important. We were together. We were a partnership. That's really all that mattered. If John had woken up one day and said, "Let's go to the courthouse," I would have done it. And I think he would have done the same for me. Neither of us woke up and said that, so we never did. I know married couples, both straight and gay, who don't like each other. Some hate each other. Everyone has reasons to stay coupled (or not). I sometimes hear their frustration, their anger, their vitriol. People have said to me, "I'm just trying to run out the clock until the kids leave," or, "Divorce is hard enough. I can't imagine someone you actually love dying." Most jarring, someone actually said to me, "Well, if my wife died, it would solve my problem." Yikes. John and I were lucky. We stayed together because we loved each other. But we also stayed together because we liked each other. We enjoyed each other's company. We had fun together. We had adventures together. There was never a moment that I thought, *I don't want to do this anymore.*

In twenty-one years, John and I had exactly one fight. Of course, we got irritated with one another, but there was only one fight. We owned a business, and it was a business fight. I was an asshole. I own it. I don't remember exactly what the issue was, but I am a type A personality and John was a type Z. At that moment, I didn't think he was "trying hard enough," and I had a meltdown. He told me the next day that if I ever talked to him like that again it would be our last conversation. And he was right. Nothing was worth a fight, especially a business fight.

After John got sick, I started wondering if we should get married. I was very concerned that the hospital and doctors wouldn't talk to me if things were critical, and John couldn't advocate for himself. John was in charge, and I deferred to him *always* until the end. He needed and wanted to fly his own plane. But there was a nagging in me that was concerned that something would happen, and I couldn't make a decision that needed to be made. That never occurred. Even though we weren't married, the hospital put it in his records that I could be present, and they would defer to me if he was unable to make a decision.

The lack of a marriage certificate was never an issue with our accounts, money, or property. We had beneficiaries named or held joint accounts. Properties were deeded in both names with right of survivorship. We were okay with not walking down the proverbial aisle. Our relationship is what mattered. Our partnership is what mattered. We didn't declare "in sickness and in health." We chose to live it. We chose to make that commitment each day.

A Hair Model

Did that man, John, have some hair? And it was *good* hair, too. It was thick, wavy brown (with gray speckled in as he got older). In college when we all did crazy stuff, John did a couple of hair modeling gigs. I'm told he also had an eighties rat tail, a la Duran Duran. *Eye roll.* Maybe if I'd had hair like that, I would have had a rat tail, too. I lost all my good hair in my twenties.

John asked the oncologist early on if he would lose his hair. She didn't know. "Some people do. Some people don't," she explained. John really didn't seem too fazed by it. But I wondered, how was he going to handle it deep down if his hair started falling out? He and his hippie personality handled it just like he handled everything. After the second round of chemotherapy, his hair started gradually thinning. Then small clumps began coming out. He hadn't yet lost too much of it when one day he called me out on the back patio. He said, "Get the clippers. We're cutting it all off." And that was it.

John was a great-looking man with great-looking hair. After we shaved his head, John was a great-looking man with a bald noggin. He never mentioned his hair again. When John paused chemo to do the five weeks of radiation, his hair started growing back. It was very fine and very thin. Now that was funny. He thought so, too. He didn't ask me to shave it. He let it grow. I called him my bald baby bird. He was cute.

Chemo started back up after five weeks of radiation. His baby bird hair fell back out and he was back to being a great-looking man with a great-looking bald head.

A New Normal Life

John came home from the hospital in January 2022. The next few months meant figuring out what our normal was. We had to figure out our new way of living. John was wobbly at first and used a walker to regain his strength. Immediately after surgery, his neurologist ordered physical therapy. The therapists came to our home for a few weeks, but after he got stronger, John was released to outpatient physical therapy at a clinic. By April he was working again. There were chores

John, at home a few weeks post-surgery, January 2022

around the house that he was capable of doing. He started driving some. We settled into a pretty routine way of being. It was up to me to keep the ship running, but John could help some. I was grateful for whatever he could offer. He could put dishes in the dishwasher. He could pull weeds in the garden. He could vacuum. That man loved his vacuum. Even though we had a robotic vacuum, John believed the robot vacuum didn't clean as well. He was probably correct. If he wanted to vacuum again, I wasn't going to discourage it. It was a way he could contribute. John didn't have an overtly assertive personality, but he had incredible tenacity through his cancer journey. He made the most of every day, and he committed to making a contribution every day.

As he was gaining his strength back, it was in the dead of winter, so we really didn't go to too many places. The weather was frigid. We would go to his doctors' appointments and chemo treatments, but John was fairly home-bound. His oncologist had gotten John approved for a "temporarily disabled" hang tag for the rear-view mirror of his vehicle. John would say, "Just because I can't use my arm doesn't mean there's something wrong with my legs. And besides, walking will help build up my endurance." Never once in three years did he let me park in an accessible parking spot and throw up the hanging tag.

After John gained some strength, momentum, and confidence, I started sometimes going places and doing things without him. He would do the same. In September, I had tickets to see The Shins with some friends. He had an appointment for a scan that afternoon. Unless I had an important conflict, I always took John for scans and any appointment when he would see a doctor. His appointment was at 5:00 p.m., and the test was scheduled to run an hour. I thought there was a chance I might be a little late and might miss the opening band. But usually, things went pretty quickly, and I really anticipated getting there on time. We arrived at the hospital. They took him back pretty quickly. He was gone for an hour. Then he was gone for two hours. I asked about his status at the desk. They said the schedule was backed up. He was gone for three hours. We rolled back home at 9:15 p.m., and then I needed to get some food in him. It was the only time in three years of caregiving that I had a full-blown meltdown. I was full of sadness and rage. I wasn't angry at John. He knew I was upset, but I tried to do a good job of holding it together until I got John in bed. My emotions around John's terminal illness came flooding out over missing an insignificant rock show. In three years of taking care of him, that night was one of the few times I cried. There were many reasons I cried that night. But mostly, I cried about the death of my once-normal life.

The Party's Over

There is a byproduct of grief that I didn't expect. I expected loneliness. I didn't expect the work it takes to be with people. In my younger years I was high on the extrovert scale. As I've grown older, my extroverted personality has waned. In social settings, I'm fully aware of the energy it takes to be engaged, to be funny, to be a good listener, to contribute, to be a good friend. I now realize, when John was around, it was so much easier to be with people. I had back-up. He might tell a story that I had heard a million times, and I didn't have to listen. He could tell a dumb, but cute, joke. He would engage our friends. I wasn't checked out, but we were each responsible for fifty percent of the entertaining. That's now gone. I'm now one-hundred percent, and it can be exhausting.

I have friends who are worried that I'm breaking up with them. The overused phrase, "It's me, not you," rings true. When John was sick, we saw people a lot. People wanted to help. They wanted to take care of him. He wanted to see friends. Now that John is gone, my friends want to take care of me, too. I'm not yet in a place to be cared for. My soul wants solitude. I desire stillness. I need quiet. No one can heal this deep wound. No one can replace the part of you that is gone forever. Maybe it grows back. Or maybe you just get used to that part of yourself being gone. I need space to heal.

When John died, the social balloon deflated for me. My ability to connect was stunted. I can still pull it together. But our friends got comfortable showing up to the continuous party. Now, that party is over. I can be social. I need to be social. But I want it to be easier. Friends will ping me. "How are things going?" "What does your week look like?" "We should get together." What I really need is to not be the cruise director. I need, "Hey. What does Wednesday or Thursday look like? Let's meet for dinner at blah-blah," or, "I'm having a couple of people over on Saturday. If you feel like it, I'd love to see you." I realize that's a departure from who John and I were. I know that's different from who everyone knows me to be. But I need a sabbatical from being in charge of the merrymaking.

Home of Popeye

It's a hot summer day in the Midwest. It's 6:30 a.m., and it's already 82 degrees. My river porch time in Chester will be limited because of the heat. It's me, my morning coffee, the Mighty Mississippi, the beautiful view, and God's creatures flying and running about.

Around these parts, it seems no one pays any attention to the Mississippi River. It's a monument that has always been there, and those who live around it cease to see and experience it. Most St. Louis residents don't give a second thought to the Gateway Arch. To them, it's that big stainless-steel structure that's just always been there. I would guess Parisians have only a slight regard for the Eiffel Tower. It's the same with this river. The St. Louis riverfront is devoid of development. There is nothing to bring people to the banks. In Chester, historically there was a longstanding stigma toward those who live by the river. Because my house is on the bluffs, I would have been called a "river rat." Or it would have been said that I "lived under the hill." Neither of those were meant to be compliments. The courthouse is at the top of the bluff, and the town developed east from there. That was the desirable direction of town. My house is south of the courthouse. But I love living under the hill, watching the river flow.

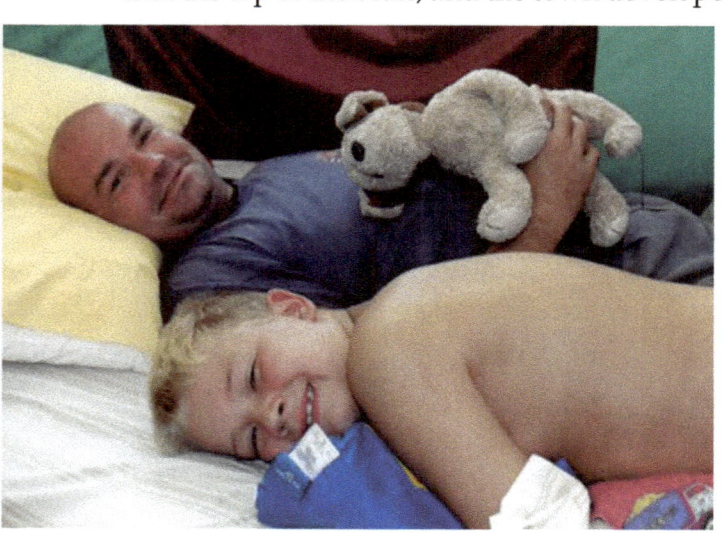

Liam, bottom, and me camping in the Chester yard during major home construction, circa 2004 (photo by John)

Chester is the "Home of Popeye." Elzie Segar, the creator of the Popeye comic strip, was born and lived his early life in Chester. The characters from Popeye were

LOVE, JOHN

based on real people around town. Segar also lived under the hill. The residents of the time were fishermen, boat hands, and dock workers. The river rats were the working-class people who labored on the river.

The Mississippi is one of the most famous rivers in the world. Mark Twain's Huckleberry Finn and Tom Sawyer cruised

Cardinal Christmas gift from John's sister-in-law, Debbie, December 2024

this river. It was the setting for *Show Boat, Mississippi Burning, A Time to Kill,* and *O Brother, Where Art Thou?* But most importantly, the Mississippi is a source of life. It serves as commerce, as drinking water, as transportation. It sustains wildlife. It sustains human life.

I know how incredibly lucky I am to be having coffee, looking at the Missouri farm fields, watching life flow from that river. It is truly awe inspiring. I know how lucky John was to experience that. And I know how lucky we were that we got to experience it together. There are so many birds. There are so many cardinals. Lore tells us when you see a cardinal it is a visit from a loved one that has passed on. In a song by Kacey Musgraves called "Cardinal," she sings about a visit from a cardinal bird that is bringing her a message from a loved one who passed away. It was on pretty heavy rotation on our satellite radio station when John was undergoing treatment. John used to say, "When I'm gone, I'm not coming back as a cardinal. That's bullshit. There can't be this many dead people flying around. It's just not possible." Then he'd giggle.

The Christmas after John died, his sister-in-law, Debbie, gave everyone in the family a gift of a ceramic cardinal with the words, "always with you" printed on the side. On the tail, she wrote "John 9-14-24." Debbie didn't know that John refused to be reincarnated as a bird. I have since told that story to Debbie and the rest of the family, and we laugh about those ceramic cardinals just as John would have wanted. I have mine on the sill of the kitchen window that overlooks the river. I just walk by and smile. John's not flying around out there as a cardinal. But he's smiling with me, sitting on the windowsill.

The Cancer High School

In mid-summer 2024, John's brother Kevin started experiencing nasal congestion and sore throats that wouldn't go away. Kevin had never had his tonsils out. After examining his throat, the doctor thought his tonsils might be infected, necessitating a tonsillectomy. Subsequent doctors' visits indicated Kevin possibly had throat cancer. John was in his third year of treatment, and it looked like his brother might also have cancer. After undergoing an MRI, those scans showed some abnormalities on Kevin's lymph nodes. Two biopsies were taken and sent for results. A PET scan was then performed. In August, a month before John died, Kevin was diagnosed with Mantle Cell Lymphoma. Kevin immediately started chemo at BJC/Wash U where John was also being treated.

John and his brothers grew up in St. Charles, MO, a suburb of St. Louis. John's parents bought the first house in a brand-new subdivision in the late '60s. They lived in a new subdivision, and the soon-to-be westward population explosion from the city to the suburbs in this area was in its infancy. Houses were new. Schools were new. There was a lot of open land.

John and his brothers went to school at Francis Howell High School on Highway 94 in Weldon Springs, MO. The school district purchased the land for the high school in 1949 from the U.S. Federal Government under the War Assets Administration.

Three miles south of the high school currently sits the Weldon Spring Conservation Area, an 8,400-acre tract of land owned and managed by the Missouri Department of Conservation. During World War II, the area was home to a chemical plant that produced trinitrotoluene (TNT) and dinitrotoluene (DNT) and processed uranium. Chemical waste was stored on site. In addition to the chemical plant, the Conservation Area was home to the Weldon Spring Quarry. The quarry was used by the Army for burning waste material from explosives manufacturing and disposal of TNT-contaminated rubble. Soil and groundwater became contaminated. In the early-to-mid-1960s, the Atomic Energy Commission used the quarry to dispose of both drummed and uncontained uranium, thorium, and radium residues from the chemical plant and from a uranium processing facility in St. Louis.

In 1984, the Environmental Protection Agency proposed listing portions of the land on the National Priorities List due to contamination with radioactive waste. A portion of the site was added to the National Priorities List in 1987. Another portion of the site was added to the National Priorities List in 1990. Kevin graduated from Francis Howell High School in 1980. John graduated from Francis Howell High School in 1982. John died in 2024 from Ewing Sarcoma. Kevin is currently in remission from Mantle Cell Lymphoma.

Popcorn

John *hated* popcorn. He didn't particularly like the taste of popcorn, but he loathed the smell of it. If his coworkers cooked a bag of microwave popcorn, it would send him into a rant. Yet he was too nice to tell them. He'd just complain to me about it. I grew up in Knoxville, Tennessee, where there is a historic Spanish Moorish Art Deco theater called the Tennessee Theater. Many bigger cities have "Fox" theaters that are similar in style. Knoxville has the Tennessee. When it opened in 1928, it showed films. An organist played before the show and at intermission. The smell of freshly popped corn always permeates the building. Now, the Tennessee mostly hosts live music and theater. When I'm back in Knoxville a few times a year, I try to get to a show there. The year John got sick, my mother had been to a show at the Tennessee, and as a fundraiser for the theater, they sold candles. Popcorn candles. Candles that smelled just like the popcorn

John's coworkers would pop in the microwave. That year, John and I got a popcorn candle as a Christmas gift from Mom. I laughed. And I laughed a little more. There was a lot going on that year, so it was an easy conversation to avoid. John didn't know Mom had given him a popcorn candle. Mom didn't know John hated popcorn. Months and months later, I confessed to both of them. John said, "You're not burning that thing in my house."

After John's surgery to remove the growth from his neck, he was in the hospital for over two weeks. It was draining physically and emotionally for both of us. We were trying to process the cancer. We were trying to understand how his physicality and his life would be impacted. We were just trying to figure out how to live. He was on some heavy-duty drugs. He had a six-inch open wound on his neck that was cut down into the spine. When he was in the hospital, he sometimes talked a little crazy. I never knew if it was the drugs or the stress. Maybe it was sleep deprivation or worry. One late night, I looked up to see he had his eyes shut tight, and it appeared he was quietly sobbing. That made sense. He was laid up. He had the big "C." This wasn't how life was supposed to turn out. I got up, went over to him, and as pastorally as possible took his hand and asked him what was wrong. He opened his eyes and continued, not sobbing, but belly laughing. I said, "What on earth could be so funny?" He said, "See that clock on the wall? Every time the second hand strikes a number, the popcorn starts popping out of the bag. It's the popcorn clock. And I just realized I've lost my mind." Apparently, his pain medication, Dilaudid, sent him into wacky world. That was one of his favorite hospital stories. Months later, John's sister-in-law, Linda, gave him a "popcorn clock" that had pictures of cartons filled with popcorn on the face of the clock. He got a kick out of that gift. Frankly, it was a little tacky. Linda knew it was tacky, and John wouldn't allow popcorn in the house anyway. So, our compromise with Linda was hanging it in the garage. It keeps great time, and John's popcorn clock keeps me on task with a smile on my face.

The Big Lie

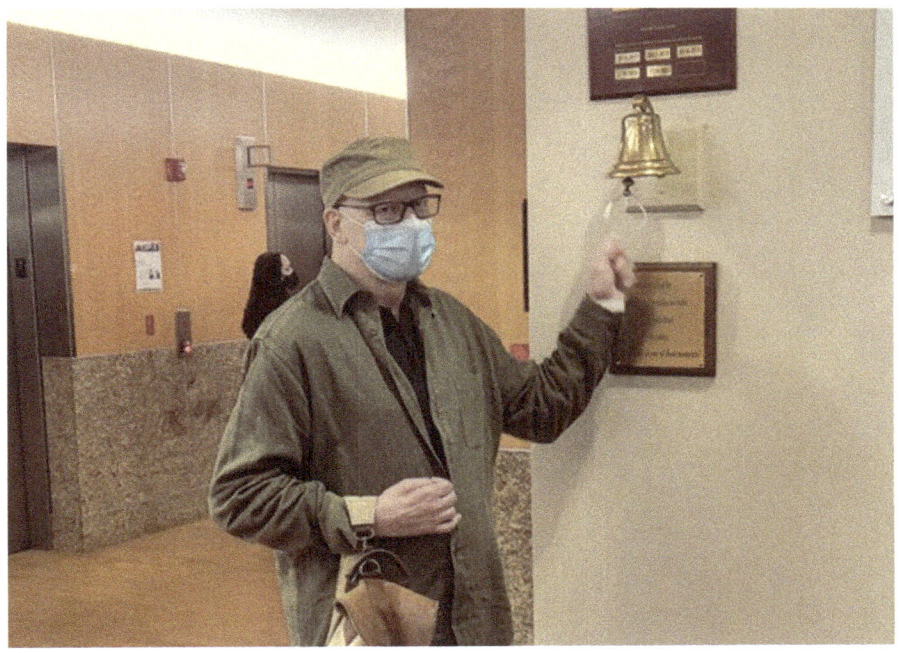

John ringing the bell "signaling the end of chemo," April 2023

John was scheduled for seventeen rounds of chemotherapy, and each treatment round began every third week. Depending on the drugs, he would either have four consecutive days of treatment, or he would have one day of treatment. That protocol alternated every other round. John had sickness and nausea, but for the most part, he tolerated chemotherapy fairly well. His first few chemo treatments were particularly rough, though. But once the docs got his nausea medication adjusted, treatments weren't horrendous. John still didn't feel well, but he wasn't miserable. It would typically take John three days after chemo to start to feel normal again. Since chemo rounds happened every three weeks, we could count on John having two good, normal-feeling weeks each month. John's oncologist was very encouraged and pleased that he tolerated treatments so well. She indicated that John was the exception and that many adults with

Party invitation photo to celebrate the end of John's treatment and return to normal life, June 2023

Ewing Sarcoma didn't finish the chemo and radiation treatments. Their bodies just couldn't handle it.

John would typically have scans after completing two rounds of chemo. That would mean he'd test for cancer progression or reduction every six weeks or so. Throughout the seventeen-session treatment protocol, things looked positive. The growth on his neck was still there, but there were some indications of shrinkage and no new signs of cancer cells. He hadn't regained the use of his right arm or hand, but we settled into a new routine over the course of those sixteen months.

On April 27, 2023, John came out of the treatment area to the lobby of Siteman Cancer Center with one of his nurses he was particularly fond of. Wearing a blue surgical mask to protect him from germs, John rang the bell to signal the end of his treatment. Our friend, Ana, was there with me. We celebrated the accomplishment of him completing seventeen chemo rounds and thirty-three radiation treatments.

Before that seventeenth (and supposedly final) chemo treatment neared, we decided to have a party. We would close the street and have a celebration with our friends, family, and neighbors. We planned a bash. We hired a band. This is the "edited, second edition" invitation that we sent:

"KICK OFF SUMMER OPEN HOUSE!"
Saturday June 10th 5-9 p.m.

We planned to celebrate the end of John's chemo. But we jumped the gun a bit. Turns out John has a little bit of cancer that popped up and will still need treatment. But the party goes on! We appreciate all the support the last year and a half and would love to see you. Kids welcome and if we missed someone, please invite them. Some food and a basic bar provided. Feel free to bring something to share or a cooler, but it's not necessary. We're closing off the block north of Hartford until 9 p.m. Bring camping chairs and cross your fingers for good weather.

The Jenny Kavanaugh Band plays from 6-8

LOG, the band plays 8-9

We'd love to see you.

The party was amazing. John referred to it as his "half-time show." Instead of it being the end of treatment, maybe it was only half-time. Family came in from out of town. Friends he and I had known for years showed up. We couldn't have asked for a better evening. I have no idea how many people were there. It was definitely over one hundred, but I can't venture a guess. There were lots of people. Lots of people loved John. Lots of people love me. I am so grateful for that night.

A few weeks after John rang that bell, he went in for the next set of regular scans. This time, the results showed cancer cells and growth in the tumor. He said he wished he'd never rung that bell. It was a big lie.

Crystal Ball

I was with a friend of ours about a week after John's surgery. She was telling a story about seeing a psychic a few years back. I don't recall the details of who or why, but she was really intrigued with the reading she got. She asked me if I thought I would want to see a psychic. I was slightly intrigued by the idea. But I was puzzled that she asked me if I wanted to get a reading. I remember asking her, "Why would I want one?" She replied, in reference to John's diagnosis, "Don't you want to know?"

During John's first oncology visit after being told he had Ewing Sarcoma, his physician explained the disease and treatment and the path forward. It may sound crazy, but that's all I needed to hear. I'm not sure if I even Googled it. If I did, I just did it for quick reference. I certainly didn't do a deep dive. I didn't read survival, remission, or recovery statistics.

I didn't "want to know." I didn't want statistics to tell me. I didn't want a psychic to tell me. What good would come of the knowing? I got up every day and did the best I could. It wouldn't have changed what I did or how I treated him or how I interacted with the world around me. What the future held was irrelevant to our present-day journey.

A few weeks after the party and after knowing the results of the scans, John had his regularly scheduled oncology appointment. The doctor put him back on the same chemo treatment schedule and asked, as she always did at the end of the appointment, if John or I had any questions. John asked her, "What's my prognosis? How much time do I have left?" She responded, "I don't have a crystal ball. No one knows the answer to that question. But statistics would tell us you have one to two years left."

Baking with Julia

The first summer after he got sick, John was perusing cooking recipes one day, and he came across Julia Child's video series *Baking with Julia,* season three (1997). It is a fascinating watch. At the time of filming, Julia was 85 years old. She wore a red blouse with a navy-blue apron and a heavy gold necklace with matching earrings. She spoke in that high-pitched voice with her odd cadence. At least in this video, she very much had a drag-queen quality to her. In the episode, her guest chef was Markus Farbinger, and he showed the viewers how to make a warm poppy seed torte with poached apricots, a Viennese pastry special.

Our friend Jen was eager to join the afternoon's kitchen festivities. The apricot poppyseed Austrian bake was on. We all watched the video together and agreed it was a beautiful cake. John wasn't much help, but he was right there in the middle of the action as Jen and I created our own Viennese specialty cake. We started by poaching the apricots. We creamed spices with butter and eggs and made a meringue that acted as a leavening agent or baking powder agent. We mixed the meringue into the bowl with creamed butter, and then we folded

Austrian poppyseed cake featured on Julia Child's Baking with Julia, July 2022

cake crumbs and ground poppyseeds into the wet ingredients. The recipe called for 2.25 cups of poppyseeds (and no flour). Essentially, the poppyseeds acted as a "flour" and a thickening agent. We poured the batter into a cake pan and placed apricots on top of the batter. We baked then dusted it with powdered sugar. We cooled and plated it. The cake was stunning. The crumb was dark, almost black. The orange apricots and powdered sugar gave a beautiful contrast to the dark pastry. It was a work of art.

When Julia tasted Chef Markus' poppyseed torte, she remarked in that high-pitched, odd voice, "Mmm. Mmm. I've never tasted anything like that before at all. I think this was a fascinating cake, and it's so beautiful to serve. I think there was apricots, and then there's very special flavor. I've never tasted anything at all like it before; that kind of that sweet, slightly acidness of the apricots. And the…it's really, I think, a masterpiece I would say. It's so beautiful. And then having a really classical Viennese cake brought back to life again. I think it's just a great achievement. Thank you very, very much."

Of note, Julia Child never said it tasted good. And we had noticed the nuance and laughed about it before making the torte. We cut the cake. We served it up. We all took a bite. The room was totally silent. We each took another bite. More silence. As Julia said, "There's this very *special* flavor." After yet another moment of silence, we all burst out laughing, because it truly had a very special flavor. We sent some cake home to Jen's pre-teen kids. Children eat anything, right? We thought, *Maybe they'll like it.* Her daughter said after one bite, "I don't hate it. I just don't want it anymore. Can I put it in the garbage?" Jen's son said, "It kind of tastes like dirty socks smell." When Jen gave us the children's reviews, John roared.

Finding the Meaning

Before John got sick, I thought I had a pretty good idea of the meaning of life. I believed life is about creation. We create to hopefully make things on Earth better for ourselves and those around us. Some people procreate and have children, others create music. Some people restore houses, others create art. Some people grow a garden, others build airplanes. Some people write poetry, others upholster furniture. Some people design skyscrapers, others write memoirs. Maybe partly, the meaning of life is respecting what those before you have created. There is meaning in respecting, caring for, and re-creating what someone has poured their heart and soul into producing. And there is importance in respecting and caring for what God has created.

What, then, is the meaning of life when you watch deterioration and destruction instead of creation? That was a very difficult question for me as I watched John's decline. Just because his body was failing didn't mean that there weren't amazing moments of clarity and growth and awe and inspiration. Certainly, that is creation. But I want to win. I want the creative energy to produce results and not just personal growth. I want the end product to be the best. If the result isn't the best, that offers an opportunity to get better, to do it better the next time and give yourself an opportunity to be the best. With caring for John, I only had one shot. And it was an unwinnable game. We knew that, but that knowledge didn't ease the feeling of total defeat and demoralization.

I hope John somehow experienced growth and creation during his illness. I never really asked him that question. John's cancer made me better. It made me slow down. It made me more thoughtful. It made me more compassionate. It forced me to create a peaceful home

46

environment where John was as comfortable as humanly possible. John made me a better man. But guilt permeates that growth. Why did John have to pay the price of his life for me to become a better man? I'd give it all back to have him back. The only thing I can do now is stay better and to try to continue to create.

The (Non) Memorial

"I don't care what you do," John remarked one day. "I'll be gone. I'm donating my body to Wash U. You need to do what you want for yourselves. If you want a party, have a party. If you want a service, have a service. But anybody who wanted to come and see me had years to do it." He had lots of time to decide what kind of service or memorial he wanted when he died. He spoke about it with both his family and me. John also believed the "half-time show" block party we had a year earlier was his living memorial. He got to see all his loved ones.

I didn't want a service, a party, or a wake partly because of John's feelings. Mostly, though, I was completely and utterly exhausted from the last three years of caregiving. I was drained from the last six months of deterioration and the last four days of complete chaos. I just didn't believe I could get it done. I was completely aware of my weakness. I didn't think I had the strength to greet his friends, my friends, his family, my family and help them through their grief. Services are for "closure." But for whom? Mourners that "show up to support the family" are saddled with their own grief and sorrow. I just wanted to sink into silence to find solace, not help others through their grief. Neko Case wrote a haunting dirge called "South Tacoma Way" included on her *Furnace Room Lullaby* record from 2000. A portion of the lyrics are, "I didn't make it to your funeral. / I didn't want ritual or resign." Later the song continues, "Couldn't pay my respects to a dead man. / Your life was much more to me."

John's family gathered at our house the afternoon after he died. I remember asking everyone what they thought we should do about a memorial. They all knew John's opinion. Most everyone put in their two cents. Oddly, the family was ambivalent about a celebration. I turned to John's son, who hadn't said much, and said, "Okay, Liam. Do you want to have a service?" He said, "You know, I just feel like we are doing that now."

We didn't have a funeral or a memorial. A few weeks after John died, a group of our friends who knew John before we met had a happy hour at a bar to celebrate John's life. I couldn't go. I was spent. I didn't want to hear the stories. I didn't want to tell the stories. I may have lost friends that day. But I had already lost the most important friend I had.

Aunt Nancy

John loved his garden. He knew what and where to plant. Since he only had the one good arm, he couldn't really plant anymore, so he'd just order me around. That was fine. I didn't mind. He was better at landscape design than I was anyway. I learned a lot from him over the years and am consciously and constantly trying not to screw up his garden. Even though he was limited, he still loved being outside, and he could pull weeds with his one good hand. We had the most weed-free flower beds in the universe during his health journey. I was proud of his beds, and I was proud of him for continuing to contribute.

One evening, John and I were invited to Ana's house for dinner. Years earlier Ana's Aunt Nancy had given her a poinsettia plant for Christmas. After the plant bloomed that year, Ana kept it around, watered it, let it grow, and it became part of her household landscape. It bloomed once a year with those beautiful red petals. She named her poinsettia "Aunt Nancy." John and I arrived at Ana's house that evening as she was picking parts of Aunt Nancy up off the floor. Ana had knocked the poinsettia over, and there were several broken stems strewn about the dining room floor.

John, adding a project to my to-do list, thought maybe we could take some of those stems, root them, and see if we could get Aunt Nancy to grow at our house, too. The real Aunt Nancy was full-blooded Cuban and spoke with a heavy accent that Ana loves to imitate. She had passed away a few years earlier. Being older and from a different culture, Aunt Nancy's politically-correct sensibilities were somewhat lacking. She knew Ana had a lot of LGBTQ friends but would still call gay people "the fruits." Yes, that was offensive, but we all laughed about it. None of the three of us ever got too worked up about anything. And John was the least likely to be offended. John and I researched how to propagate a poinsettia from a stem. The internet, which never lies, says you just stick those stems in a pot of soil, keep it out of the sun, water sparsely, and the plant will root. Putting sticks down into dirt didn't seem like a recipe for success to either of us, but we followed instructions. After a few months, that poinsettia exploded. Ana would come over to visit and say, "Yeah, Aunt Nancy loves living with those fruits." Of course, John would laugh. Aunt Nancy bloomed beautifully last February and stayed red until May. Aunt Nancy didn't bloom for the fruits at Christmastime, but I like to think John smiled at her red blooms in February.

Watermelon

John loved watermelon. I bought a watermelon today from a guy selling them off of a trailer on the side of the road. What am I going to do with an entire watermelon?

I don't want to forget that John loved watermelon.

The Waiting Room

Throughout John's almost three years of treatment, we became very proficient at waiting. It seemed as if each half-hour appointment required a three-hour calendar block. A quick doctor's visit was just not possible. John gained a little strength after his spinal operation in December, 2021, and he was scheduled for his inaugural chemotherapy treatment lasting five consecutive days from Thursday through Monday the following February. There was no way to know how his body would react to the poison being pumped through his veins, but he was given medication to help alleviate the nausea. He kept food down the first two days, but as the treatments continued, John got sicker and sicker. He was given nausea medication intravenously during chemo, so he never got sick at the hospital. When he came home each day from treatment, however, nausea flared, and John was miserable. We messaged the oncologist's office. But it was the weekend, and we got no response. Monday was a federal holiday. John just had to tough it out.

John had an appointment with a neurologist on Tuesday morning after his initial five days wrapped up. For the previous three days, he hadn't held any food down. He was weak. He was shaky. I asked him if he wanted to cancel the neurology appointment. He replied, "It'll take forever to get back in if we cancel it. We have to go." I loaded him into the truck.

The BJC hospital complex is expansive. Supported by his walker, John shuffled slowly along the hallways until we arrived at the neurologist's office. The nurse greeted him with, "Hello. Name? Date of birth? Insurance card?" He feebly muttered his name and date of birth. I handed her his insurance card. After a few moments of typing, "Can I get a signature giving your consent for treatment?" came next. I glanced at John. His body was moving in a circular motion. His eyes were rolled back. I ran behind him, put my arms around him, and caught him just as he was tumbling forward. The nurse said, "Is he okay?" I didn't answer her. I just said, "We need a wheelchair." In no time, an orderly appeared with a wheelchair, and I gently guided John back into it. The nurse said, "Don't worry about it. We don't need the signature. You can have a seat in the waiting room."

I rolled John into the packed waiting room. Another nurse rushed over to us and brought a cup of water. John thanked her, took the water, and swallowed a few sips. She turned to go back to her post, and John said to me, "I'm going to vomit." I jumped up and told her we needed a bucket *now*. With milliseconds to spare, John heaved into the pan that had just arrived. The nurse turned to me and asked, "Is he always like this?" I curtly answered, "No. It's the chemo." Though the waiting room was full, within five minutes a door opened and another nurse called John's name. I wheeled him into the exam room with his recently cleaned plastic pan lying on his lap. The door closed. With his eyes completely shut, John muttered to me, "Well, I guess we know the secret to getting in and out of here."

The Buying Spree

After he didn't get remission, and cancer cells around his tumor started showing up on his scans, John resumed his regular treatments. The tumor wasn't growing rapidly. His oncologist started offering suggestions of experimental protocols. John followed all the rules, and if his doctor suggested he try something, he was game. In the fall of 2023, he started one of the experimental treatments. One of the side effects of the new medication was that blisters could form on his palms or the soles of his feet. After a week of taking the medication, his feet started badly blistering. And it happened quickly. It was excruciating. He couldn't walk. That first night of blisters he crawled to the bathroom. He'd cry trying to stand up to get to the toilet. The next morning, I searched Facebook Marketplace and found a transport wheelchair for him, so I could wheel him around without him trying to walk. To greatly exacerbate the problem, he had gone to his son's house the week before to help him in his yard. He pulled and cut down Virginia Creeper (akin to poison ivy) and had a severe breakout with blistering on his arms, hands, and face. This wasn't a result of the medication because his reactions to the weeds began before he started the experimental medication. It was a horrendous month. I remember going to the drug store to get something for his ivy rash and running into a friend of mine. He asked me how John was. I didn't say it out loud, but I thought to myself, *Well, he's still alive, but I'm not sure he'll live through the weekend.*

While the purchase of the wheelchair was several months before John started his rapid decline, it was the beginning of the panic-stricken buying spree. There was no guidebook on how to make things easier or more comfortable for John. He wanted to be as upright and functional as long as possible. Our nurse friend Ana likened his deteriorating physical condition to someone with ALS, except he had cancer. She would give suggestions to facilitate eating and drinking. I bought utensils with thick diameter handles on them. For a short time before losing complete function, he could still grip with his left hand. I then bought dinner plates with a raised edge along the perimeter so he could push his food over to the side of the plate and onto the spoon. I picked up straws so he could lean over and drink without picking up the glass. I ordered insulated hard plastic "on the road" cups with lids that had a rubber bottom that wouldn't slide. I could put those on a table or on the flat arm of a chair, and he could bend over to take a drink. There were still spills occasionally. One week, I ran to Target and bought kids' sippy cups. John never got angry. But he was pissed about that one. I quickly took them back. Trying to keep us both as rested as possible, we didn't sleep in the same room. But the bedrooms were next to each other. He would call for me at night if he needed me. One day, thinking it could be beneficial, I borrowed a baby monitor from the neighbors. Again, John was not pleased or happy with a baby monitor. After I bought plastic straws, we found them to be too flimsy. I then bought metal straws. Then I bought metal straws with a bend in them. I put bidets in the bathrooms. That made his bodily functions easier on both of us. I bought foam tubes that spoons or pencils or toothbrushes could be inserted into to make them easier to hold. It was a year of playing Whac-A-Mole. It seemed every day was another crisis to solve. The solution that worked for a few days quickly became obsolete for us. The only solution that seemed to help was bourbon.

Performance Improvement Plan

John and I both liked to have "treats." Especially after John got sick, five o'clock was treat time. They weren't dog treats, ice cream treats, or candy treats. They were adult treats: cocktails. John wanted to see his family and friends, and treat time was fun for him. Yes, John was on chemo. Yes, John was on pain meds. But there came a time when I decided I would give John anything he wanted. I never wanted to parent him, but being conscientious about his health was always at the forefront of my mind. At some point, though, his mental and emotional health became more important than his physical health. Physically, he wasn't going to get better. He wasn't going to live through this. My goal was to keep him as comfortable and content as possible. No one could take his cancer away. No one could take his pain away. But those around him could just be with him and make him smile. We could help him feel loved. If John wanted to have 5:00 p.m. treats with his loved ones, that was as important as his chemo treatments.

John had his bloodwork tested the morning before he started each chemo treatment. He'd say after each blood draw, "How do you think my liver numbers will come in?" I don't know how, but they always showed up in the normal range. He was convinced the chemo was protecting his liver, killing those bad cells. Neither John nor I specifically asked his docs if he could or should be drinking. I would occasionally make mention of happy hour in his appointments and never got pushback. During one oncology appointment, I mentioned a cocktail and said, "I figure at this point, John can have whatever he wants." His doctor smiled, raised her eyebrows, and gave me a nod. She never said anything, but I took that as a green light.

The week before John died, my mother was in town from Tennessee helping out. I had tickets to see ELO, my favorite band as a teenager in the seventies and eighties. I had never seen them and was pretty pumped. It was also a perfect evening for me to escape for a couple of hours. At that point, John wasn't walking well and used a wheelchair. He could sit and stand with some assistance, but his decline had become more severe. Before I left, I told Mary, "Listen, feed him whatever he wants. If he wants bourbon, give it to him. Give him anything he wants." I traipsed off to the show. A couple of hours later, I sauntered back into the house. Mary had gotten John loaded. He was chatty. He was half-sensical. It wasn't a problem he was shit-faced. The problem was getting him out of the recliner and into the wheelchair to get him to the bathroom and then into bed. He was 170 pounds of pure dead weight held up by what was normally very wobbly legs and was now drunken wobbly legs. The next morning, I told Mary I was putting her on a PIP (Performance Improvement Plan). She said, "You told me he could have anything he wanted." That was true, but we still had to get him in bed. The three of us had a good laugh.

After John was forced to retire, the days for him got long. He could no longer turn the pages of a book or magazine. He'd watch movies and listen to music. But he also fancied crime shows. For a time, John loved the show *Dateline*. One day, he called me into the living room and said, "Turn that shit off. I'm not watching that anymore." I replied, "Why? You love *Dateline*." He came back with, "It's always the spouse. They try to trick you and make you believe it's somebody else, but it's always the husband or wife." He was so pissed he literally never watched a crime show again.

Treat Time would come. I'd pour him a bourbon. I'd put the rubber-bottom cup on the flat arm of a chair he would sit in, and he would drink from a straw. He'd usually have two. Sometimes, he'd ask for a third, but usually not a fourth. When he'd venture into bourbon number three, I'd say, "You better not die on me tonight. They'll do an autopsy and find out the bourbon killed you. They know you can't use your hands. I'll go to prison because it's always the spouse." Then he'd say, "I'll have another treat." And with a big smile, he'd continue, "Just tell them it was our neighbor, Jen, that poured me that drink."

Anger

Many times, I talked with both John and his family about the fallout that would happen after he passed away. I was convinced that some people in his family, if not all of them, would hate me. When people die, tension overwhelms those remaining. Anger reigns. There is mistrust. Death can bring out the worst human qualities. Families fight over money. Families fight over trinkets. Families fight over funeral plans. Families just fight. I didn't prepare for a fight because it takes two to battle. Whatever anyone wanted to fight over, they could have. John was very clear about his wishes. He was very clear about his finances. He didn't have directives about the little things. But anyone in his family could have anything that was John's. To me it was just stuff. I had my experiences with him. I would have my memories. If they wanted a watch or a ring or a shirt or a painting, they could have it. They could take anything they wanted. They all vehemently denied they would be angry at me. They did turn angry, just not with me.

In grief, anger consumes people. Death is an unexplainable hole that can't be understood or filled. The anger can be pointed at a target that seems logical and sensible but is really just random. People don't know what to do with their emotions. Some of John's family members have created a canyon between themselves. Some have cut contact with each other. I'm sure there were family issues before John died. John's illness put a tourniquet on the bleeding. After John left, previous issues combined with grief, raw feelings, and helplessness around John's death may have led to these rifts.

I love John's family. They all held it together when John was sick and because John was sick. Everyone got along well enough. They probably did it for him. When John died, the keystone fell out and sparked the already smoldering embers to ignite a raging fire. What is lost by cutting a relationship? What are the consequences? We lose common experience, shared love, potential for new adventures, and most importantly, potential for growth. We lose the ability to have love and support during crises like being diagnosed with a terminal disease. There are good reasons to opt out of relationships. Everyone must draw their own lines in the sand. Some reasons to end a relationship register a number ten on the scale. But some register a two. Is it worth termination because of a two? It's everyone's prerogative to choose their own people. Successful relationships must be loving, life-giving, and forgiving. Human relationships are imperfect because humans are imperfect. The propensity to judge is a prevailing human condition. Those judgmental tendencies are both learned and innate. The judgment is difficult to overcome. John's family pulled it together for him for a quick minute. They gave up being right for a quick minute. They had a common goal for a quick minute. Forgiving each other is the greatest gift they could give John. He'd say, "Let's just have a treat together."

Circus

In August 2017, there was still work to be done on the Chester home. John's and my gut-rehab renovations, largely on the weekends, resulted in a tortoise-slow pace inching toward completion. However, the house featured a nice working bathroom with a shower. Cold air efficiently blew through the HVAC vents. Art hung on newly installed painted drywall. And the figurative circus was coming to town.

Many parts of the United States would experience a solar eclipse on August 21, 2017. Chester would be in the path of totality. The region was hyped. Neither John nor I were science geeks. We knew what an eclipse was, of course. We knew people were excited. We both thought, *Okay, is it really that big of a deal?* Yes, it was *that* big of a deal.

While St. Louis had a short window of totality, the southern portion of the region experienced a much longer period of darkness. There were many people from the St. Louis region who drove south an hour and a half to the communities around Chester. The closer it got, the louder the talk got. The excitement was building. A couple who was friends of John's family "reserved a room" with us several months in

John, left, and me at the first solar eclipse in Chester,
August 2017

advance. He was an air traffic controller. That made sense. He was a
sky and science guy. But as the day approached, we started getting
calls and texts from family and friends and St. Louis neighbors. "Can
we come?" Okay. Sure.

A week or two before the event, a little panic started to set in.
There are very few parties that John's family will miss. John had a
niece coming in from Indianapolis. His brothers and their families
booked the short road trip. Traffic from St. Louis to the southern
region was expected to be heavy. To make sure they didn't get stuck
in traffic, a few friends and John's family came the day before for an
overnight. After it had all shaken out, there were 15 people staying
overnight. The Chester house has two full beds, one twin bed, and
one bathroom. For the eclipse event, I made sure the Chester house
had a newly rented and very attractive blue porta-potty sitting beside
the driveway.

When we got the final sleeping count, I put my foot down. I told
John his family had to pitch tents outside. Their family always took
a yearly camping and float trip, so sleeping in a tent wasn't foreign

to them. "This is a small house. Nobody sleeps on the floor. They've got to be outside in tents," I declared. The eclipse day was August 21. Everyone set up their tents the day before as planned and as instructed. 10:00 p.m. rolled around. It was 81 degrees. 72% humidity. No wind. Everyone crawled into their tents, lying in their vinyl sauna shelters. The first floor-sleepers showed up in the house at 10:15. Within two minutes, all the Jenga blocks fell. The tents emptied. There were sweaty sleeping bodies covering the entirety of hardwoods. John's family was in the house. Everyone was together. Looking back on it, I'm glad.

More friends showed up on the actual eclipse day. There was food. There were drinks. The worry du jour was the weather. It wasn't predicted to be a rainy day. But would there be clouds? An eclipse party without the sun or the moon is just day drinking. A few of the surrounding Chester neighbors had eclipse parties as well. The next-door neighbors had scientist friends who had traveled from Germany for the event. Eclipse goers migrated and floated from party to party. As the moon inched closer to the sun, the clouds floated away. The sky was completely clear. As a non-science-geek who didn't understand the hype, I found it to be an awe-inspiring natural phenomenon I'll never forget. The moon began blocking the sun just before noon. It started getting darker and darker. At 1:20 p.m. totality was achieved. The moon covered the sun. People cheered like they were at a football game. Kids squealed. A couple of people cried. Birds started singing. Cicadas started buzzing. Crickets started chirping. My Chester eclipse family was transfixed for two minutes and forty seconds. It was a once-in-a-lifetime experience.

Circus II

Or maybe not.

The once-in-a-lifetime 2017 eclipse experience actually became a twice-in-a-lifetime experience. Solar eclipses are a very rare occurrence in the same viewing spot. In 2017 the viewing path crossed the United

States from Salem, Oregon, to Charleston, South Carolina. That path ran right over Chester and Southern Illinois. Coincidentally, six and a half years later, on April 8, 2024, Chester was in the path of another solar eclipse that spanned from Maine to Texas.

John, middle, with brothers Ken, left, and Kevin, right at the Chester solar eclipse, August 2017

Since almost seven years had passed since the last solar eclipse event, our family and friend dynamic had shifted somewhat. The younger kids in John's family had grown up. Some were away at college; some were now out of college. John was also sick and battling cancer. This time, things were different for the moon's trip in front of the sun.

John and I planned to be in Chester for the eclipse, but we decided not to have a party. People hadn't been asking to come, probably due to our circumstances. This eclipse would be chill, with just us. But a couple of weeks before it occurred, we had neighbors who are good friends ask if they could come to Chester and bring their family. His father is a science teacher. He had an uncle who was flying in from the Pacific Northwest for the event. They wanted to find a great watch spot. Of course, they could come to Chester, we said.

As it got closer, some more people inquired. Not surprisingly, another gathering materialized. We were ready. We were seasoned eclipse party planners. This gathering was lower key. The night before, we had guests at the house, but everyone had a bed. No bodies on the floor. No tents in the yard. Afterward, we had one lone friend stay over.

The worry of 2017 was rain, clouds, and heat. The worry of 2024 was rain, clouds, and cold. Early April can be chilly. We readied the food. We prepped the drinks. And, of course, the people showed up. There weren't as many people as in 2017, but we probably had 50 people there. This eclipse started around 12:42 p.m. and lasted two and a half hours. Total darkness lasted three minutes and twenty-five seconds, fifty-five seconds longer than darkness in 2017. The sky was clear. The temperature that day was 79 degrees. The day was perfect. The gathering was perfect. Everything was perfect, until it wasn't.

As we were setting up tables for food and getting ready for the party, John mentioned to me that he was having numbness and pain in his left arm, his usable upper extremity. Throughout his treatment, each day brought new issues and challenges. Side effects from medication were prevalent. A new symptom wasn't unusual, but I could tell he thought this might be different.

The eclipse was on a Monday. Both of us went back to work on Wednesday. John was concerned about the numbness in his good hand, but he worked the rest of that week. He had a trip to Nashville planned with some friends the upcoming weekend. The Floating Men, a band they used to see in college, had scheduled a reunion concert. I wasn't invited. Or maybe I declined the invitation. I thought it would be a good chance for him to be with other people without me. It would be a good chance for me to decompress and have some alone time. Ana went with him on the Nashville trip, and they shared a hotel room. They said the band was amazing. I talked to John several times that weekend, and he told me the numbness in his arm was getting worse. Ana helped him button and unbutton his jeans all weekend. That arm and hand were soon to be useless, too.

John and his friends got back to St. Louis on Sunday evening. On Monday, April 15, 2024, John called his manager. He never worked again.

Cream of Mushroom Soup

John was so polite and so kind. He would have never intentionally said something to offend. The rare times he inadvertently offended someone, he apologized profusely and was bothered by his hurtful words. Those who knew John well knew he liked to cook, and he sometimes had valid, but private, critiques. He was, well, a food elitist. Meals didn't have to be chef-prepared. Ingredients didn't have to be exotic. But if he or I were cooking, the ingredients were fresh. We rarely opened a can of vegetables—or, really, a can of anything. Dishes were seasoned well. Food was plated on ceramic flanked by a cloth napkin. He'd say, "We have to do laundry anyway. Why wouldn't we use a nice napkin?"

Some food trends were deal-breakers for John. Campbell's condensed cream of (fill-in the blank) soup was one of them. He wouldn't even eat condensed soup as actual soup. For him, casseroles made with it were particularly vile. Years ago, we attended a friend's potluck. One of the guests unveiled a "cream of" casserole. She and I were face to face, but John was behind her. He looked directly in my eyes and began to feign vomiting. I averted my eyes and conjured up the saddest image possible to prevent a burst of laughter. He later said, "Why would anybody eat that gelatinous bullshit."

A month or so after John's spinal surgery, Ana thought a MealTrain page could be beneficial for us. The MealTrain site organizes a schedule for friends and loved ones to bring meals. She thought it would be helpful to take some pressure off of me, and it was an opportunity for our friends to contribute and show their love. We set it up to have meals delivered once a week, on Wednesdays. John was still very weak from surgery. When I told him about the MealTrain, in a tone barely above a whisper, he said, "Great. Cream of chicken casseroles." Then he gave me a feeble smile.

Several friends later asked me, "What was the worst thing somebody brought over?" That's a fair question that I would probably ask, too. Honestly, we didn't really have a bad meal. My guess is that people who couldn't cook elected to bring carry-out, so the food was always great. It's possible Ana gave very specific instructions about condensed-soup dishes. One day John remarked, "I guess this is what it's like to be a senior citizen getting Meals on Wheels. You just never know what you're going to get."

The MealTrain was an amazing contribution, but it drove me crazy. Part of the problem was Covid. The pandemic was raging. John didn't feel great. Our friends didn't know how to navigate us, nor did we know how to navigate them. They didn't know if they should drop the food, knock, and run. They didn't know if they should knock, come in, and say "hello." It was a strange for someone to bring something for us and not have any interaction with them. Before cancer and Covid, friends would be over all the time. Now, John and I weren't sure if we should invite them in. As time went on and Covid restrictions were relaxed, some friends did come in, but we didn't know if we should stay ten feet apart. Sometimes John felt good. Sometimes he was in bed, and he wondered if he should get up and be gracious because someone was bringing dinner. Some people who brought food were really close friends while some weren't. Some people forgot their day. Some people brought it on a different day. The forgotten days or the different food days weren't bothersome because we always had food in the house, and there were lots of days that John didn't eat much anyway. John and I both had pretty good social instincts, but this was awkward-as-hell territory. I'm so grateful for the effort and the kindness. I'm also glad I ended it after four months. I had enough on my plate to organize. Managing the MealTrain was low on my priority list.

Paperwork Hell

In April, 2024, John was already on FMLA due to needing time off for treatment. But he was still a full-time employee and had been working since recovering from his surgery two years earlier. Being a federal employee has its pluses and minuses. His pay wasn't the best, but he had good benefits and good insurance. The most important piece of the puzzle for him was good insurance.

Over the years, and even before his diagnosis, I would ask him questions about his benefits or retirement. He would always say, "We don't really have an HR department. I'll ask my manager, but there really isn't anybody to call." That was unbelievable to me. I would sometimes think he just wasn't really motivated to get the answer. During his cancer ordeal, I would mention the lack of information to his coworkers, and they confirmed that no, he can't just call the HR Department. It didn't really make sense to me.

John retired on a Monday, but he retired without any preparation. Most people apply for retirement weeks or months before their expected date. John didn't have that luxury. He didn't plan on retiring that day. He was 60 and was vested with the federal government. He had 16 years of service and, thus, was eligible for a pension. We began the navigation of the Federal Retirement System and the Social Security Administration. His manager at his agency was able to direct him and get him a representative at the Office of Personnel Management. If there was a handbook about how to accomplish this, we weren't aware of it. His OPM counselor was a big help, but you couldn't just give her a call. The process involved emails and applications. John's government email and computer access was soon to be cut off. To add to the chaos, John couldn't use his "good" hand anymore, so he couldn't just log on to his email.

Sometimes I am thankful to be living in the twenty-first century. I did many Google searches trying to figure out the process of getting him retired. Since he was employed by the government, all that information is public. It may be convoluted and confusing, but it's out there. Because John, a federal employee, was retiring due to a disability, the rules were different than if he simply retired. Before he could submit his retirement paperwork, he had to apply for Social Security Disability benefits through the Social Security Administration. Although I'm not completely sure of the reason, the amount of his social security disability payment affected the amount he would receive for his pension. Since both payments were from the federal government, the amount of his social security benefit would be deducted from his pension. Maybe getting both payments is considered double dipping. It didn't matter why. We just needed to get the ball rolling.

John's inability to work was stressful on him because there was less money coming in. But financially we were fine. John had some savings and had gotten an inheritance when his dad died. I was working full time. The money was the last thing on my list of worries. Like many of us, in John's earlier working career, times were lean. Especially after his divorce, he shared custody of Liam and was a single parent. We also previously owned a business that had very thin financial years, particularly early on. Frugality was baked into John's psyche. He wasn't exactly cheap, but he always had to watch his "pennies," as he would say. Not only was he concerned about his lack of financial contribution to the household, John also was concerned that, at some point, he'd have to move from the house and into a facility for care. He knew that would be very expensive. I was confident that would never happen. I considered the possibility of bringing someone in to help, but I never thought he would move from our home.

The first course of action after he quit work was to apply for Social Security Disability. Everyone has "heard" the stories and has seen the commercials about getting denied for Disability. "No one ever gets approved for Disability on their first application," is the prevailing thought. We heard that over and over. John wanted to hire a lawyer to help us with the process. We had a phone appointment with an attorney and explained John's situation. He essentially told us that he'd be happy to help with the application, but he saw no reason why we couldn't do it ourselves. We could do it more quickly than his schedule allowed. He also believed there would be no reason that John would be denied, even on the first application. We decided to follow that path, and the attorney said if we ran into issues, he'd be happy to pick it back up.

We started the disability application online. I, of course, filled out the application with John's input. It was cumbersome. We attached medical records. We answered employment questions. We answered family history questions. After we completed the application, I clicked submit. A pop-up window appeared, and the message said, "Due to the nature of your disability, please visit one of our Social Security Administration offices and bring your completed application." This wasn't exactly happy news, but we would do whatever we needed to do. Later that week, we showed up at a field office, waited our turn, and John's name was called. John gave the nice woman at the counter his name and social security number. She typed it into her system and said, "We asked you to come in because I just needed to confirm you have a terminal illness." At this point in John's journey, most people could probably have looked at him and assumed that. He briefly told her that he had Ewing Sarcoma cancer and had a malignant tumor on his spine. She looked at his paperwork, typed a few things into her system, and replied, "In cases like this, we require a site visit, so I can fast-track your application and get you approved ASAP." We were both pleasantly surprised. About a month after John's visit to the social security office, he got a letter stating he was approved for Social Security Disability. The letter went on to say that there is a five-month waiting period before he would receive benefits. His first direct deposit would arrive on October 22. His response was, "I've worked and paid into this system for forty-two years. If it's the last thing I do, I'm going to get that check." He didn't get that check.

Since he had applied for disability benefits, John could then submit his application for federal retirement. That application was even more burdensome. I think when it was complete, the application was about sixty-five pages. Much of that application was physicians' statements and his medical records, but it wasn't an easy assignment. He and I also had to make decisions regarding disbursements. For instance, since he had a terminal illness, he could take a lump-sum payment in lieu of his monthly pension. That sounded like it could be a reasonable option. But when the calculations were completed, I believe the lump sum was around $8,000. I think his monthly pension would be about $2,200. John said, "Surely, I'll live more than four months." There was also an option to leave the pension to a spouse but at a reduced rate. We weren't married but could have gotten married. Briefly we talked about it, but nothing came of that. Planning a wedding was hardly an efficient use of our time. And, honestly, I didn't want John to think

I wanted his money. No one knew how long John would be alive. Making these decisions was like playing the roulette wheel. When someone is alive and breathing, there is always hope for the next day and the next day. It was possible that John could have drawn his pension for five more years. There was just no way to know. In hindsight, we left money on the table. John and I were making the best business decision we could without having a crystal ball. John also should have taken that lump-sum pension check. We just didn't know.

After the retirement application was submitted, John got a letter indicating he (or really, I) didn't fill out a portion of one of the sections. I, as his proxy, filled it out quickly and mailed it back in. We were lucky that we were both college-educated. Completing all the paperwork took some smarts, but even more importantly, it took sheer will and tenacity. There are so many people who wouldn't be able to get the retirement application or the disability application completed. About six weeks after the resubmittal of the amended application, John got a letter stating he was approved for retirement effective May 1. It would take some time for his calculations to be ready, but he would receive retirement benefits from the date he was approved. The first payment would be in a lump sum to pay him for the first few months he was approved. Then, a regular monthly direct deposit payment would begin. After he received his approval letter, a burden was lifted for him. Again, financially, we were stable. The process was just so hard. I don't think we talked again about his benefits after everything was approved. I had access to all of John's accounts because his hands were inoperable. I would occasionally look at his bank account or credit card statement. He still paid for things, so I made sure everything looked okay. But I really didn't look often. As his condition worsened over the summer, his retirement benefits were somewhat forgotten. A week after John died, I logged into his bank account. Five days before he passed away, John had gotten his first and only retirement pension payment in a lump sum. I'm not beating myself up, but I somehow wish I had seen that and told John he was officially a paid retiree. He would have been thrilled.

Badass Mary

My mother, Mary, is in her eighties and lives in Tennessee. Mary is a complete badass. She goes to the gym most every day. She walks and walks and walks that poor dog of hers, Freckles, dragging her all around the city of Knoxville. While Mary is in great shape, John and I believed we should have a plan in the event Mary needed, or wanted, a place to go as she got older. I've seen many families struggle because a parent is amazingly self-sufficient at eighty-five years old. Then at eighty-five and a half, they can't get to the bathroom by themselves. Around the time John was completing his chemo regimen and hope was in the air for remission and a path toward normalcy, John and I bought a house across the street from our St. Louis home. Purchasing that house was an insurance policy for the future. We deemed it "Mary's House."

The home is a two-story, 1,425-square-foot Craftsman-style built around 1910. While the bones and structure were good, it needed extensive rehab. From time to time, eighty-year-old Badass Mary would come up to help. The first week after we purchased it, Mary visited. That trip was actually more than a visit. She came to help rip out the carpet and remove crumbling plaster. As she was carrying buckets of plaster to the dumpster, I just hoped nothing would happen to her. I was afraid someone would call the senior services police on me. "I promise, officer. She's really doing this by her own free will."

John had lost his mom twenty years earlier, and he really thought of Mary as a second mother. He was very protective of her and was one hundred percent on board with the purchase and rehab of Mary's House. After all, we were using our money, not just my money. He wanted Mary to be comfortable and safe wherever she lived. If she ended up in St. Louis, he wanted her close. He wanted her across the street. The two-story structure may not be ideal as someone ages in place. However, the home we lived in was a one-story with wide doors and a no-threshold shower. It could be perfect for Mary. If needed, John and I could move to the two-story. It was a solid plan. Until.

We wrote the contract to purchase Mary's House when we thought John's treatment was complete and he had gone into remission. A month after we closed, we were told by John's doctor his prognosis was one to two years. But if some people live one year, there are probably others who live three years. Right? We soldiered on. I kept ripping out walls. I kept building new ones. I kept hiring contractors. I kept painting. As the months wore on and John's condition worsened, it became clear that if Mary needed a place to retire, she could move into my house with me. We wouldn't need Mary's House.

John died a year and a couple of weeks after we bought Mary's house. A month or so before he left us, he wanted to go see the progress. A friend of ours and I took him over. He was still walking, but he was very wobbly. We held onto him as we slowly guided him up the five front stairs into the house. There were also stairs that led to the bedrooms on the second floor. I remember him saying, "Of course I want to go upstairs." We got him up those steps. And we got him down. I knew that would be the last time he would see Mary's House.

That year before he died, John couldn't physically help me with the renovation, but he had always been a source for support. He had always been a sounding board. He was there to prevent me from second guessing. After John died, I continued to work on the house. That fall and winter my motivation was understandably stunted, and I didn't labor as hard as I could have. As winter turned to spring, I had regrets about wasting that time. Finishing the house just didn't seem that important anymore. John was no longer there to tell me, "I think the sink should go over there instead of here," or, "This isn't the right color for this room." Sometimes, I just needed to hear him say, "Bill, that looks really good." I know if something looks good or needs improvement. But it's reassuring to hear it from the person you trust most. That's gone.

John's family would come and stay with him toward the end. When John's sister-in-law, Linda, would come over, they would get on the laptop and look at Zillow. They were Zillow buddies. They laughed at the horrible décor people had in their homes. They critiqued the kitchens and the colors and the landscaping. They marveled at the hoarder houses that were on the market. It was fun for them. When Linda or others visited, I would often go across the street to work on Mary's House. I was gone, but I was still close if something happened or they needed me. Working on the house gave me something else to think about and focus on. After John died, working on the house kept me moving and kept me doing something productive. Even though I wasn't as task oriented as before, working on the house became an escape. It became my therapy.

John has been gone eleven months. Mary still exhausts her dog walking the streets of Knoxville. She won't need that house. Mary's House goes on the market next week. I'm really proud of what we accomplished there. As the project neared completion, I was very surprised by the emotional uprising it caused in me. I don't know why. Maybe it was another chapter door being slammed shut. Or maybe I just wish John were here to see it. I wish John were here to know what we accomplished. I wish John were here to know what an amazing venture he was part of. I wish John were here to pull it up on Zillow with Linda. With a beautiful kitchen, impeccably designed bathrooms, sleek furnishings, no clutter, and smart landscaping, John and Linda would surely deem it the Zillow champion.

A.J.

Our 1946 Streamline Modern commercial building that we converted into a single-family residence is unusual in a Victorian/Arts and Crafts-era neighborhood. The building was built on grade with the sidewalk, and there are no steps leading into the front door. It is an easy house to navigate. It is accessible for someone with mobility issues, but it is also visually accessible through big commercial windows that look into the living room. While the windows have a tint, people can see in if they are visually purposeful. When John initially came home

Portrait sketches by our artist friend, A.J.,
August, 2024

from the hospital, our neighbor made curtains for us. Our neighbor and I thought John might want privacy. He really didn't. At first, we would occasionally close the curtains, mostly if someone was sleeping on the sofa in the living room. Neither he nor I really minded people looking in. We didn't do anything racy in that front room other than watch cooking shows and *Dateline*. We also knew all the neighbors. The open windows didn't bother us.

Because the windows go floor to almost ceiling, sitting in the living room gives one the feeling they are sitting outside in the front yard. Snow storms are stunning, and you feel like you are centered in a shaken snow globe. Spending time in that front room, John saw everything that went on in the neighborhood. The openness kept him connected. Often John would say to me, "There goes Darrell walking Cleo (the dog)." Or he'd say, "Katie's getting DoorDash again."

One day, three weeks before John died, I was out working in the yard. A small, older Asian man whom I had noticed before but didn't know walked by. He stopped and, in a very thick accent, introduced himself. He told me he was Japanese and his American friends call him A.J. I could tell he was a character. It was difficult for me to understand everything he was saying. He liked our house. And he could see the art inside. He told me he was an artist and would very much like a tour of our home. I gave him a polite, "Oh, sure. One day maybe I'll show it to you." I didn't think too much about that interaction. A few days later, I got a note in the mailbox from A.J. with a sketch of the house showing me exactly which paintings he wanted to see and asking for an appointment. He then included his phone number and asked me to call and set a time and date.

When I told A.J., "Sure. Maybe one day you can see the house," I thought that would be the end of it. I hadn't mentioned to John that I had met this A.J. gentleman until I showed him the note. John said, "What? You surely aren't going to let this man in our house, are you? He could be a serial killer." Remember, John was very fond of Dateline. I said, "Listen. He's harmless and a character. He's little and old. We can take him." John replied, "I can't use my arms and I can barely walk. I don't think we can take him." Then I said, "Okay. I can take him. But he just wants to see our art. And how does he know we aren't the serial killers?"

A few days later, A.J. showed up at his appointed time. We invited our friends Jen and Sue over for the afternoon. They are always up for an adventure. I got everyone a drink of their choice. It was a little early for "treats," so I think everyone drank water. We also didn't want to be tipsy if A.J. was, in fact, a serial killer. I gave A.J. the nickel tour, then invited him to the living room for a chat. The afternoon was an absolute scream. I have no idea if A.J. is sixty-five years old or one hundred and sixty-five. Reasonably, he's somewhere in between. But he's a very well-preserved older man. He told us in an accent that took some concentration to understand that he came to the U.S. to live in New York in the seventies. Jen's mother-in-law was Japanese, so Jen was our translator. A.J. would say something in a heavy Japanese accent. Jen would repeat it in a bland midwestern accent. I felt like I was at an improv show.

A.J. told us he was an artist and recounted that, when he first came to New York, he was a sign painter on billboards and buildings. He said when the painters were up on the scaffolding and they needed to go to the "little boys' room," they would just pee in a bucket. When it got full, they'd just lower it down with a rope, empty it, and send it back up again. He explained his artwork had been exhibited in some New York galleries. We later leaned on Google to confirm. He came to St. Louis for love, but those (two) marriages haven't worked out. He smiled a lot at our friend Sue, and we were all sure he was smitten. He said he keeps in shape by jumping rope, something like 2,000 rotations a day. He was very eager to show Sue the videos of himself jumping. While those videos were impressive, they weren't enough to get him a date.

A.J. continued to say he had a final art installation idea that he wanted to exhibit, but so far, there hadn't been a gallery willing to accept his project. He said that, when he dies, he wants his nude body to be cut in half. Both halves would be pressed between glass and displayed. We all sat silently for that story. I think Jen may have even stopped translating. The afternoon came to a close without any murderous activity.

The next day, the four of us got a text from A.J. "Bill, I enjoyed your art collections and being with your partner and friends. When you have another seasonal installation in your house, please let me know. I might bring my ex-wife who got her own house recently and is interested in how people create interior of their house (yours should be a nice sample for her)." In addition to the text, he sent a "cartoon drawing" of the four of us and labeled each person. I responded, "Thanks for coming over for a visit! Did you make our faces better than they really are?" Sue chimed in, "I have bangs." Jen retorted, "I think we can all agree who has the least flattering portrait of all…. I have a bit of a sneaky look. I think that's accurate." "You're making me laugh," wrote Sue. Jen closed with, "Very lovely to meet you A.J.!!"

Sue subsequently got a text or two with some videos of A.J. jumping. To my knowledge she hasn't had a date with him. John had a ball that zany afternoon.

John the Tree

While John's personality lent itself to him being on the slow double-decker sightseeing tour bus, I'm typically on the bullet train. Very shortly after John passed away, I started going through his "stuff."

John and I had already performed a good purge of his 60-year collections when we moved him into our new house from the hospital after his spinal surgery.

John's cousins came in from Ohio a month after John left. They were close cousins and had traveled to St. Louis the year before to see John when he was sick. When they came back after John died, I had had a gathering with them, John's son, his brothers, and his nieces and nephews. While John had made it known that he didn't care if we had a party, this was the memorial that John would have wanted and approved of. Our St. Louis house is a half a block from Tower Grove Park, a beautiful Victorian park. John loved that park. In his last few years, he walked it several times a week. His legs functioned until the very end. It was one of his favorite activities and a way to be independent. He could get out of the house and have some time away from me. As a gift, his Ohio and Pennsylvania cousins had a tree "dedicated" to John there. The tree is a young London plane tree in the sycamore family. It was an amazing gesture. I now walk by "John" several times a week. I know he's not there, and I don't need a reminder of John. But even though I don't need a reminder, it's nice to have one.

The cousins came to the house that weekend. We walked to the park to see "John the Tree" and take pictures with him. We ate. We drank. We laughed. We cried. John had a lot of pictures, old-school printed out at Walgreens. He apparently was quite the photographer in the years before we met. He had copious amounts of family photos of a young Liam and nieces and nephews. I never once saw a camera in his hand. But when we met, technology was changing, so we always had a "camera" available.

That weekend, I put hundreds of photos on a table. The family pored over them, reminiscing about them. I told everyone to take what they wanted. As I had been going through John's things, I started pulling some items out for his family. I thought they might like to have reminders also. I wrapped up things of John's that I thought could be good remembrances: art, jewelry, home goods, clothing. I don't remember what all was in those boxes. Hopefully, what would just be "stuff" for me became welcome reminders of John.

*John's high-school
senior photo, 1982*

School Photos

One of John's things I came across after he died was a framed collage of John's school pictures from first grade to twelfth grade. It was *so damned cute.* But what am I going to do with twelve of John's school photos? Was I really going to hang this thing on the wall? Apparently, John didn't think it went with our home's aesthetics either because it was in a box in the garage, and I had never seen it before. But it did make me smile.

As great as the pain and despair of losing John is and was, I am also fully aware of the suffering this has caused our families and our close friends. Shortly after his death, I sent condolence cards to family and some of our close friends. It was healing for me to acknowledge who he was for them. It was important for me to honor what they had with John. I lost a partner. They lost a father, a brother, an uncle, a best friend. I hurt for myself. But I also hurt for them. I love them, too, and wanted to acknowledge their hurt and grief. It was also a great way to get rid of those school pictures of John. Each got one. After the serious sentiment, I would write something like: "You get goofy fourth grade John who apparently didn't get his hair combed that day."

The world is constantly changing. Things that were important half a generation ago seem not so important anymore. In the days, weeks, and months after we lost John, I received a number of condolence cards. It was so healing for me. It was incredibly comforting to know that people shared my sadness and sorrow. It was heartening to me that they recognized and honored John because I don't want them to forget who he was. Cards came from our friends. Cards came from John's medical teams. Cards came from people that knew John that I didn't know. Many of the cards were religious in nature. Some were inspirational. One card sported the simple phrase, "Well, Fuck!" A card came from the next-door neighbor boys, five and two years old. They drew pictures. They glued things onto the paper. The "card" read, "We're sorry John died. He was an important man." What people shared in those cards gave me a glimpse of the senders and who John was for them and who I am for them. I believe some were trying to reconcile John's death with their own ultimate and impending mortality. Some were trying to understand the role of God in a world of suffering. Some were grappling with the age-old question, "Why do bad things happen to good people?" They were reconciling their sorrow. They wrote to assuage my grief and their own.

I don't typically keep birthday cards or Christmas cards. I appreciate the sentiment. It's nice that someone thought of me. Keeping almost 60 years of cards can pile up. But I kept those condolence cards. Those who sent them shared their hearts with me. Their sharing opened a door for me to learn about them, about John, and about myself. In a year or two, those cards may mean something different to me. I may have a different perspective. In the future, there may be something else they can teach me. Or one day, I may have learned all I needed to learn from them. That's the day they will go away. For now, I treasure the cards.

Neko Show

Neko Case tours regularly. During the course of his three-year cancer battle, John saw two of her shows. He regularly announced he wanted to see her one more time before he died. I thought maybe if Neko kept touring, we could keep him alive. The summer that John was declining quickly, I bought tickets to a Neko show that was scheduled in St. Louis in September. I really thought we could make this happen. I knew this time would be the last. Several weeks before the show, I emailed Neko's manager and told her that John was really sick, and he wanted to see her show one more time before he died. I thought maybe the band could do a shout-out to him or something during the show. Neko's manager was very kind and said they would try to reach out as the show date got closer.

Meanwhile, John was deteriorating. I had four tickets, but I started getting very concerned I wouldn't be able to get John down to the seats. In the weeks before the show, I grabbed a couple of accessible tickets so that, should he be in a wheelchair, I would be able to get him in and out. The show was at a small, historic, acoustically amazing venue, The Sheldon Concert Hall and Art Galleries. The theater seats 700 people. Even though the accessible tickets were behind the floor section, every seat in the house is incredible. Since I picked up two more tickets, I asked John's brother, Kevin, if he wanted to go. He said he did. He had been introduced to Neko's music when John was sick in bed and asked Kevin to play her music. Kevin really began to enjoy her music as well. The concert plan was set. Kevin invited a friend and would sit in the regular seats with our two other friends. John and I would sit in the back where it would be easier to navigate. As the concert drew closer and we were within a couple of weeks of the show, it became clear that John would need to be in a wheelchair. I had made the right move buying two more tickets.

On Monday, two days before the show, I got an email from Neko's manager that said, "Hi Bill, we were able to put you on our guest list as a gift from us. Also have a soft item, like a hoodie or T-shirt

that John might like? Can we gift him something cozy? Our tour manager is on here and can help with any additional access you need at the venue." My reply: "Hey Guys. Thank you so very much. John left us on Saturday. While I'm not surprised, I was hoping we'd be able to get him to the show. Also, if they would want to know,

L to R: John's brother Kevin, our friends Julie, Ana, Kally, and me at the Neko Case concert five days after John died

let the band know that he asked me to put on Neko music in the hospital room on Friday. Some people may say 'it's only songs' but music was important in his life. I'd like to acknowledge that. Again, I appreciate your efforts and I will see you on Wednesday."

I didn't know until months later, but in the hours before John died and I had left the hospital to go home and get some rest, John told Kevin to turn off the music. If John had said that to me, I think I would have known he was close to the end. The five of us went to the show that Wednesday. The tour manager found me before the show and gave me a tote bag with a ton of artist merchandise and a condolence card from Neko. It was a really special gesture of generosity and kindness that I will cherish always. There was an empty seat down by my friends, and they wanted me to come and sit by them. I didn't. I stayed up in the accessible row. They were concerned about me and kept suggesting I move. Finally, to shut them up, I told them I wanted to be in my seats so I could "sit up there with John." That wasn't true. I wanted to be alone because I was barely present that night. I wasn't sad or angry or grief stricken. I was…. Just. So. Tired. I dozed off during parts of the show. After the concert, one of my friends asked if I "liked the song Neko dedicated to me. It was her new song, the spider song." I heard the spider song. I didn't hear a dedication if there was one. I was too tired to listen that night.

When I was giving away some of John's things to his family and they were going through his clothes, Kevin told me that if I ran across a Neko band shirt of John's he'd like one. I told him I didn't think John ever had a Neko shirt, which was the truth. For Christmas, I gifted Kevin one of the band shirts that the Neko team had given me. In that bag there were a couple of shirts, some patches, and stickers. There was a baseball cap. There was also a "bookmark" promoting her soon-to-be released book titled *The Harder I Fight, the More I Love You*. In the bag was also a sticker with a drawing of a wolf's head. Above the wolf are the words, "Everything's Gonna Be Alright." The bookmark and sticker are both taped up in the interior of my bathroom medicine cabinet. I read them every day.

Never the Same

My friend Jen is a musician and songwriter. Before John got sick, she wrote a song for a family member who was having health issues. The song is in my Amazon music library, and through the years when John was sick, it would randomly play. I never discussed it with John. I don't know if he ever really listened to the words.

JUST THE SAME
By Jenny Kavanaugh

When the world starts crumbling down; all the pieces lie
around you.
And you feel you can't be found in the rubble that
surrounds you.
You won't be the same, never quite the same, and I will love
you just the same.

I take you as you are so go on and fall apart. And I will piece
you back again.
You remember the things you did when you were a kid
and dreaming.
And you don't know how to be that now; how to work
somehow and start believing.

And you won't be the same. Never quite the same and I will
love you just the same.
I take you as you are so go on and fall apart and I will piece
you back again.
It's time to believe in things you cannot see. And things that
just might be down the road.
I don't love you for what you do. I don't need you for things
you give me.
There's a light that shines in you. It's gonna shine right
through and start the healing.
And I won't be the same. Never quite the same. And you will
love me just the same.
I take you as you are. So go on and fall apart and I will piece
you back again.
I take you as you are so go on and fall apart and we will piece
you back again.

I'll never be quite the same.

Blow-Up Characters

John didn't start chemotherapy immediately after surgery. His
oncologist wanted to give him a little time to recover from his spinal
operation before injecting him with poison. He had come home
from the hospital in mid-January and was slated to start chemo
mid-February. His first treatments were to start on Thursday for five
consecutive days through the weekend and included the following
Monday. John's first day of chemo arrived. While he had gained
strength since his operation five weeks before, John was still weak and
didn't feel one hundred percent. His body handled the first two days
of chemo relatively well. Part of the medication included anti-nausea
meds that could be adjusted as needed. Thursday and Friday weren't
great days for him, but he powered through. He was being poisoned
after all. On Saturday his nausea became worse. Sunday was a full-on
vomit-fest. That weekend, he couldn't hold much of anything in his

John surrounded by co-workers after chemo treatment, February 2022

stomach. I messaged the oncologist's office, but it was the weekend and Monday was the President's Day holiday. It was an absolutely miserable three-day weekend.

John's last day of work before his emergency surgery was December 17, 2021. When he got admitted to the hospital the following Monday, he called his manager and went on sick leave. John liked his job. He liked his co-workers and the team he was on. He had been at his job for thirteen years and had developed good friendships. His co-worker friends were, of course, very worried and concerned about him. In the span of a few weeks, he had had a spinal operation to remove a malignant tumor, was diagnosed with cancer, and began chemotherapy. Of course, they wanted to do something for him.

A few weeks before John started his first chemo routine, his manager from work called me and had an idea. She and some other friends would be off work for the President's Day holiday. She asked if I thought it would be okay for them to come to the house for a quick visit. I agreed. According to the schedule, he should be back home after lunch. They wanted to surprise him. What a nice gesture. What could go wrong?

John had nausea meds that he took all weekend, but they really weren't working for him. As was his nature, John pressed on. He sucked it up and just dealt with it the best he could. I took him to chemo on Monday morning. The nausea seemed lowest in the mornings.

But as he was pumped with the drugs, the nausea intensified as the day went on.

His co-workers planned lunch at a neighborhood restaurant and waited for me to text them to let them know we were on the way home from the hospital. All morning, I wondered if this was a good idea. I couldn't call them off now. They had planned their day off around John. But I also needed to protect John.

When we were leaving the hospital, I texted his friends and told them we should be home in about twenty minutes. I got John in the truck. He looked ashen. After a few minutes on the road, I glanced over and his face had morphed into a dull shade of green. He told me that I might need to pull over so he could vomit. I was absolutely panicked because I knew there was a group of his friends waiting at our house. He wouldn't want them to see him like this. After John got diagnosed, I always kept a stash of purple barf bags in the car, just in case. He closed his eyes trying to will the nausea away.

When we got a couple of blocks away from home I said, "John, I need to tell you something. And I'm really sorry. I need you to know that there is a surprise for you at home. Your work friends swore me to secrecy, but a few of them will be at our house when we get there." He looked at me with a WTF look. I told him again I was sorry and that I would get rid of them quickly.

As I turned the corner and we drove up the block, I saw people. Lots of people. There were maybe thirty people out on the sidewalk in front of our house. John might be sick at any moment. I was about to be sick because I let this happen. We got closer. A giant blow-up pink unicorn was holding balloons. There was a huge blue Sully monster walking around hugging neighbor kids. We saw a blue shark and a purple hippopotamus holding signs. A yellow Pokemon Pikachu danced around the stop sign. A blue unicorn with a rainbow mane waved at cars. John's co-workers had shown up in these elaborate blow-up costumes. Since it was a holiday, many of the neighbors were off work, and many of the kids weren't in school. It was a mini-circus right there on the sidewalk.

Adrenaline is an amazing natural drug. John was thrilled. He beamed. He forgot he needed to vomit. He talked to his friends that he hadn't been able to see in several months. Their effort of love and friendship was a beautiful, bright gesture that cast a light on an otherwise miserable weekend. John visited with them for about an hour before I shooed them away. We both laughed as we watched those ridiculous characters walk back to their cars a few blocks away. John said, "Well, just another normal, typical day in south city." I helped him get inside. I put the flowers they had brought on the dining table. I put the balloons in the corner of the living room. I helped John to the bathroom where he was sick for hours. He would have been sick without the party. But he had an hour of sheer joy.

Palliative Care

When John started losing the feeling in his good arm and hand and he retired from work, he knew things were deteriorating. He still took chemo treatments every third week. John wanted to stay as mobile as possible for as long as possible, and he believed the chemo was helping keep his tumor from increasing in size. He could still walk the neighborhood. He could still take a walk in Tower Grove Park. He could still go to the Missouri Botanical Gardens. The loss of function in both hands caused an adjustment. Someone needed to feed him. Someone needed to take his pants down to go to the bathroom. Someone needed to wash him and brush his teeth. He lost the ability to do many things that most of us simply take for granted. Overall, he kept himself in good spirits. He allowed me and others to help him with daily living.

As the cancer grew, John started experiencing more and more pain, mostly in his arm and neck. After his surgery and the years that followed, John always had prescriptions for pain medications. John followed all the rules. If the bottle indicated dosage three times a day every four hours, that's what he would take. And he certainly wouldn't take it if it had only been three and a half hours since his last dose. John started having pain events where he would shake and cry for as much as an hour until another pain pill could kick in. When these events would happen, I would sometimes give him a pill and tell him his last dose was exactly four hours ago. When his body was trembling and he was out of his mind in agony, he lost his medication time frame. That was a blessing, because he didn't know he was breaking the rules. As his cancer grew and his pain increased, his oncologist upped his dosage and explained to John that, within reason, he could take as much as he needed to alleviate the pain and discomfort.

At an appointment that last summer, his doctor gave John a referral to palliative care. Neither of us really knew what palliative care was though both of us had heard of it. John's oncologist explained that the palliative care doctor could help with his pain management, and there would be social support services available. She likened it to hospice and said it was often a step before hospice care. The palliative team could help manage his pain, and John could rely on them to help make him more comfortable. We had a friend who was also battling cancer and seeing a palliative care team. Both he and his partner praised the pain management medical support and mental health services their team provided.

Palliative care sounded promising. John was unable to use his hands, but I made sure John's phone was beside him at all times. We figured out how to allow him to voice activate the phone so he could answer calls or make calls and automatically put them on speaker phone. He could also text by voice activation. A scheduler called John and set up a virtual appointment with the palliative care team.

The ability to attend appointments virtually on a computer screen is a huge benefit of the pandemic. I am so thankful for that technology. John and I both attended his first palliative care appointment virtually. The physician explained a little about her practice and mentioned that she would be taking over the pain management aspect of John's treatment. John spoke about his cancer and his current challenges, and he mentioned his pain was caused by a tumor on his spinal column that had grown to affect discs C4 to T2. A social worker was present, and he asked a little about John and me and our relationship. The physician asked about John's pain medication protocol. She wanted to know how much medication John was taking and how often. She instructed John to stop taking the pain meds on a regular schedule. Instead, she wanted him to take the meds only as he started feeling pain and wanted me to track when and how often he needed them. Of course, John followed the rules.

Before John's palliative meeting, he had been on a regular dose of Oxycontin every four to six hours. After the appointment, he stopped cold turkey, only taking pain medication when he started feeling pain. The cessation of consistent pain medication thrust him into a pain crisis that lasted five days. After the pain drugs were flushed from his system, he couldn't get ahead of the pain. John saw his oncologist the week after the palliative care appointment. Thankfully, John's oncologist instructed him to resume a regular dosage, and she referred him to a pain specialist within the hospital network.

Palliative care continued each month with an hour-long discussion of what pain medication John was on and his dosage even though John was concurrently being treated by a pain management team. The continued focus on medication by the palliative doctor was terribly redundant. In the meantime, John's disease worsened, and his mental health declined. In most of the sessions, there was a social worker present, but the doctor led the pain medication-obsessed meeting with no input from the social worker. From the discussions with our friends about palliative care, from what we had read, and from the first meeting, John and I both thought we each could receive some social support around navigating his impending death. That never happened.

A few days before his last palliative care appointment, John told me he wanted to ask the doctor for a hospice referral. In order to enroll in hospice, one must stop all lifesaving treatment. That meant John was ready to cease chemotherapy. Losing the ability to walk scared John more than dying, but his legs were now starting to fail him. At his last palliative appointment, John was in bed, too sick to attend. The doctor asked me to bring the laptop into the bedroom so John could give consent for us to continue the appointment without him. The social worker was not present, and the discussion, once again, centered around the progression of the disease and his prescribed medications. I mentioned that John needed and wanted counseling and mental health services, and the doctor gave me a number to the Siteman counseling center to get him scheduled with a therapist. At the conclusion of the meeting, the doctor said, "Since John wants a referral for hospice, do you think you want to schedule another appointment for next month?" I responded to her, "No. Thank you. I think you've done enough."

John didn't live long enough to receive hospice care. After the referral for counseling from palliative care, he had one appointment with a therapist but didn't make it to a second. I don't know why the program didn't work for John. In the end it was a huge lost opportunity. Although my emotions have softened, I'm incredibly angry that we didn't call Siteman counseling services ourselves and instead wasted four months with the palliative care team. I also question what we could have done differently. In many ways, I think we did it wrong. We should have asked for what we needed. I should have spoken up. However, I didn't know what we needed. I didn't know to speak up until it was too late. We should have laid a foundation and developed emotional support before the situation became an emergency. I didn't know it was a crisis until it was too late. I was unprepared to help John emotionally with the end of his life. I failed him.

Cancer in the Wild

I went to the grocery store today. A couple of aisles over I saw an acquaintance of John and mine. We aren't really friends, but we are friendly. He is a few years older than John would be. Some years ago, he was diagnosed with cancer, and the last time I saw him he said he was in remission and was cancer free. He was with his partner at the store. I took one look at him and could tell it was back. I've been in this movie. He was thinner than normal. His skin had that jaundiced tone. He looked really old. He moved slowly.

I should have gone up and talked to them. As the old trite saying goes, "Should is just 'could' with shame." Yes. That's right. I should have gone up and asked how he was and asked how they were. I don't even know if they know that John left us. I didn't want to tell them. I didn't want to explain it. I didn't want to hear that maybe his cancer was back. I could have centered myself and done the right thing. And I should have. Should. Absolutely with shame.

Pain Management Team

In recent years, there has been big backlash against opioids and drug manufacturers. Opioid drugs have destroyed people's lives. But used for appropriate reasons, they are a godsend. Those drugs helped John lead a relatively normal life for a few years. Reading between the lines and listening to her words, John's palliative doctor was concerned about his overuse of the drugs, my possible use of the drugs, and those drugs possibly being sold or stolen. I completely understand. I understand she was trying to be the best steward she could be. But John was in a tremendous amount of pain, and although we didn't know it at the time, he only had a few months to live.

At the appointment when his oncologist put John back on a regular pain medication schedule, she also referred him to the Christian Hospital Pain Management Center. Christian Hospital is part of the network in the Barnes Jewish Christian Health System. John was referred to Dr. Chris Beuer, a trained anesthesiologist who specializes in treating pain symptoms. Due to the opioid crisis, there are media stories about pain management clinics where busloads of people show up and get prescribed opioids. There are drug addicts who find unscrupulous physicians. Celebrities and regular people die overdosing in the care of unethical doctors. This pain clinic was completely different.

John's first appointment was on a Monday. I filled out pages and pages of background information. We met staff. We met nurses. We met Dr. Beuer. He and John had a brief conversation with John sharing his diagnosis and his current pain levels. John was a half-full kind of guy. A doctor would ask him how he was doing, and John might tell them what a good week he had. I'm more of a realist and would think, "Was I drunk all week and didn't see what a good week he was having?" I was there, too, and my perception most times didn't match his. Many times, he would be in bed writhing in pain with tears streaming down his face. Then, he'd tell the doctor the next day that he had had a good week.

After the introduction, Dr. Beuer proposed installing a pain pump. A device in John's abdomen would hold pain medication. A tube would be inserted to run from the pump in his belly up his spine to the neck. That pump and tube would feed pain meds to the area around his tumor. He would have a constant flow, but when he had a pain event, I could press a button on an app installed on a dedicated phone. That would release more medication to the area. In an ideal world, John would be able to administer the dose on the phone himself. But since he had no hand usage, someone else had to push the button.

John was a processor. He had to really think things through. At that Monday appointment, Dr. Beuer suggested John come in the next day on Tuesday and have a test to see if he would be a candidate for the pump. If all went well on Tuesday, he would schedule him for outpatient surgery on Thursday. The quick turnaround was due to the doctor going on vacation the following week. Because there was no time to ruminate, I knew John wasn't completely comfortable with this. I, on the other hand, would have pulled the trigger and had him wheeled into surgery that very day. I saw John's pain firsthand, an uncomfortable witness to John's trauma and suffering. After I talked to John for a few minutes, he agreed to at least come in the next day for the test to see if he was a candidate.

I don't remember what the test was or exactly what they did to him. It was in the office in the medical building attached to the main hospital. I think they somehow tested around his neck area to ensure they could get the tube in, but I'm not entirely sure what the procedure was. The test was successful, but it sent John into one of his pain events where he was shaking and crying and sweating. It was a horrifically miserable thirty-minute recovery. Thirty minutes doesn't seem like a long time. It's a quick episode of *Friends* or *South*

Park. But when you're out of your mind in pain, thirty minutes is an eternity. Many times, when he was in pain like that, it would help to sit him up. After the procedure, he asked me to help sit him up. That didn't help, so he asked to be laid back down. That didn't help. One of the nurses got him a cold wash cloth. That didn't help. He asked for some water. The nurse brought a cup of water. He couldn't use his hands, and he wasn't sitting upright, so he asked for a straw. The nurse said, "I don't think we have any straws." With as much breath as John could muster, he said quietly, but firmly, "This is a fucking hospital. How can you not have a straw?" The nurse looked surprised and said, "Let me see what I can do." She scurried off. Miraculously, she appeared a few minutes later with a straw. That straw may have come from a used McDonald's cup. But she came up with a straw. I did my best not to burst out laughing. John would never have said something like that under normal circumstances. We got to know the nurses and staff at the clinic fairly well over the next two months. We later talked about that incident and had a good laugh about it with the nurses. John, of course, apologized profusely. At subsequent visits and with a smirk on my face, I would sometimes ask that nurse if she could get me a straw. She'd laugh.

The silver lining to the pain pump test and his subsequent pain meltdown was that Dr. Beuer and the nurses had a front-row seat to one of John's pain events. No one could know what that was like unless they were in the room with him. When some of John's family came to stay with him, I would warn them that a pain crisis might happen. They didn't understand what it was like until they were privy to the experience. While the Tuesday test was traumatic, it was successful. John was scheduled for the surgery on Thursday. I remember being there late into the evening because the doctor got called into another procedure and was running behind. There were no complications with John's procedure. The surgery with local anesthesia went off without any issues. The previous test was much more of an ordeal.

During John's three-year torment, there were human angels that showed up regularly for both of us. Every single person we encountered in the Pain Management Clinic wore a halo. They were so kind and compassionate. They really just wanted to stop the hurt. Dr. Beuer was the head of the angel brigade. I have a special place in my heart for each and every one of the people in that office.

The pain pump wasn't perfect. John still had really intense pain. But it was a tremendous asset to help control it. John went back for weekly or as-needed appointments for them to adjust the pump. The pump had three drugs in it. Morphine was one. I don't remember what the other two were. I think one may have been to control nausea. The doctor normally would use Dilaudid instead of Morphine, but we told him that Dilaudid made John a little wacko after his spinal surgery. John relayed the story about seeing the clock popping corn in the hospital when he was hopped up on the Dilaudid. Dr. Beuer said he didn't want to make John any goofier, so he filled the pump with Morphine instead.

The pump continuously pumped Morphine up to the affected area around his neck. I could administer additional Morphine through the app by holding the "phone" close to his abdomen and pushing the play button. John started on a pretty low dose of continuous pain medicine and each additional shot of Morphine was another low dose. He started on a low dose to let his body get adjusted to the new protocol. The physician also wanted to make sure the pain meds didn't make him sick. The app was programmed so he could only receive an additional dose a set amount of time after his last dose. When he first started using the pump, I believe he could only get a booster every six hours. The care team wanted to ensure he felt okay and didn't overdose. The ultimate goal was to get him completely off the pill form of opioid medication, and he would only rely on the pump to manage his pain. As he got used to the device and the medication, the clinic adjusted the pump to give him a stronger regular dose, and they reset the pump so he could receive doses in shorter intervals. It wasn't a perfect system, but it was a godsend.

There were times that John had pain events and still had to wait for his next booster dose. Those were intense moments watching the clock as he shook in pain. Someone gifted us a bottle of lavender oil for him to sniff when he was trying to hold off until his next booster pump. I don't know if that really did any good, but it was at least a distraction. While he was fighting through the pain, he could smell the lavender oil and know he would have some relief soon. Waiting on a dose of the Morphine in the pump was still better than the pills because the pills could take thirty to sixty minutes to activate in his body. I believe, by the end, John's pump was set so he could have a dose every two hours. He didn't always need it every two hours, but it was there as an insurance policy.

I am so grateful to John's oncologist for referring John to the Pain Management Clinic. In talking with Dr. Beuer and his staff, I discovered some mistrust about his field among other physicians. John and I also encountered that when he would go for scans. It seemed many medical staff were very uninformed about how the pump worked. Before John had one scan, the radiologist was reluctant to perform the test. The doctor said the magnetic scan could shut off his pump, which we knew, but the pumps are designed to restart. John's pump always restarted, and there were never problems. However, if something did happen, John also had a cabinet full of pills I could give him. I had to assure the radiologist John had an appointment after the scan with the nurse who could operate the pump in case of a malfunction. The truth is he didn't have an appointment. But I had the nurse's cell phone number, and I could call her at any time. The pump wasn't keeping him alive; it just made his life more comfortable.

It is so difficult to watch someone you love suffer so much. The pain management team made a huge contribution to John's care and wellbeing. As John's caregiver, they made a huge contribution to my life, too. I am incredibly thankful they came into John's life.

Parents

I never met John's mom. We got together about a year before she passed away. Part of that year, we were just getting to know each other. But after a while, our relationship became more serious. I don't know if John woke up one day and said, "Okay. This is it. Bill is the one." He may have just gradually grown into the idea. I knew fairly quickly I was committed to this relationship. In that first year, John wasn't ready to explain our relationship to his family. Also, that first year of our relationship, John's mother was battling lung cancer. I remember telling John the summer before his mom passed away in the fall, "I want to meet your mom. You don't have to tell her who I am, but I want to know her." It never happened. The first time I laid eyes on her, she was in her casket.

John, center, with brothers Kevin, left, and Ken, right

John was careful. John was methodical. And John was slow. It's not surprising that I never got the chance to meet his mom. It's just how he operated. It was one of the biggest disappointments in our relationship. I wasn't angry. I wasn't really even hurt. I was just saddened by the missed opportunity. My father died about six months before John's mom. John never met my father, either. He lived 500 miles away from St. Louis. Logistically, meeting my family was a little more difficult. But I was sad that John and my dad never got the chance to know each other, also. A few months after John's mother passed, he said to me one day, "I think my mom is really happy for me that we're together. She would have loved you."

At the beginning of our relationship, one of John's friends said to me, "Have you met Jim (John's dad), yet?" I told her no. She then responded with, "Well, good luck with that one." I didn't know exactly what she meant by that, but I had gotten the impression that John's dad was "old school." He was born in 1930 and grew up in a different time with different social constructs. Fairly early, John was open with his brothers and sisters-in-law about our relationship. They were, and are, totally fine with it. In many ways, but not all, our little part of the world has become a more open and accepting place for diverse people and lifestyles. But there was always just a little bit of trepidation for me around John's dad.

Brothers Ken, left, and Kevin, center, with John, Thanksgiving Day 2023

After John's mom died, John started bringing me to family functions. I liked his dad. He was a character. He was cranky. He was funny. He was a really good talker. He told the same stories over and over, and it wasn't because he had dementia. He just liked to talk. After I had been coming around for a bit, he asked one of John's brothers, "Is Bill part of our family?" His brother told him, "Yes." Jim responded, "Well, okay then." He, along with John's other family, always treated me as one of them.

Jim would give me Christmas presents. He would tell me he loved me. He was never anything but kind and gracious toward me. The brothers would reminisce about what a hard-ass he was when they were growing up and told some pretty off-color stories about their dad. By the time I showed up, maybe he had mellowed. Or maybe he had just grown into the loving man he always wanted to be. John's dad died the year before John got sick. I'm glad he and John's mom didn't have to witness John struggle during those sick years.

During the last week of John's life, my mom was in St. Louis helping with him. John was on some pretty heavy medication. And even when he wasn't on meds, John would sometimes dream and talk in his sleep. Mom said that one day, the week before John passed away, he was napping in the recliner in the living room. Mary said that John was dozing in and out, and he was talking to his mom and dad. I didn't see or hear this. Or maybe there was so much going on that I blocked it out. I have no idea what's beyond this life. I don't know if John was talking to his parents that day. I just hope they are all together again.

Nut Rolls

John liked to cook. It was one of the things he really missed when he lost the use of his arm. In lieu of cooking, he'd watch cooking shows or cooking videos. Then, he'd "suggest" dinner options for us. Watching the shows and looking for recipes gave him something to pass the time. It also gave him a way to contribute. Although, I would come into the living room as he was watching a cooking show and say, "I see you're adding something to my to-do list tonight." During some of his medical appointments, a doctor or nurse would sometimes ask John the question, "Do you feel safe at home?" The first time it was asked, both John and I were a little startled and taken aback. There probably are caregivers who mistreat their loved ones. It was a fair question, but I would tell him later that his answer to that question would determine if he got to try Jamie Oliver's newest recipe that he had put on my to do-list.

One of John's childhood Christmastime memories was the nut rolls his mom would make. All of the brothers loved them. Their mother's family was Polish and from Pennsylvania. I don't know if the nut rolls were an ethnic bake or possibly an east-coast tradition. Over the years, both John's sisters-in-law, Debbie and Linda, had made them. According to them, it was an ordeal. You needed to block off most of the day. John's and my new house had a large, well-functioning kitchen. We both loved to cook, and a nice kitchen was a priority when we designed and rebuilt the house. Right after Thanksgiving 2021, we had a nut-roll-making party at our house. Since we had a new kitchen with lots of counter space, John invited Debbie over. It would be a month before he would go in for surgery and get diagnosed with cancer, but he had already lost the use of his right arm. The recipe called for making the dough the night before. On bake day, we made a filling of walnuts, eggs, sugar, vanilla, and milk. We rolled out the dough, added filling, then rolled up each bit like a pinwheel, and baked them. The finished product should be similar in size and diameter to a rolling pin. John laughed and said, "A one arm nut-roller probably wouldn't pass quality control, but I can be the supervisor. I don't think my nut rolls would look too great." Our neighbor friend, Jen, loves to bake. She came to the nut-roll party to learn how to make the famous pastry. Some of the rolls cracked on top, which wasn't ideal. But John said his mom would call those the "cussed rolls," and they "ate just as good as the perfect ones." Personally, I really like the nut rolls...when someone else makes them. It. Takes. All. Day.

John, trying to take a bite out of his great-nephew Paxton's cake pop. Thanksgiving Day, 2023

The Cavalry

John, center, with his brother Ken, left, and me a month before John died, August 2024

After getting through his surgery in December 2021, John's next couple of years were fairly stable. Even though things went wrong almost every day, we just got used to that and adapted. John would need his meds adjusted. We'd get that done. He would need a wheelchair for a few days. Easy enough. He and I both became proficient at flexibility. Those first couple of years, he mostly could drive himself places. If he was feeling up to it, he would oftentimes drive himself to chemo. I would always go to his doctors' appointments, but for routine appointments, he would frequently go by himself. I alternated working remotely and going to the office. And John was still working. He could get himself water or some fruit. He couldn't really cut any food, but he could survive without me for short periods of time. Occasionally, he went to the grocery store by himself and pushed the cart, which added some stability to trips up and down the aisles. Grocery shopping was a great activity if he was only picking up a few items.

The real spectacle started that April day when he lost feeling in his "good" arm. Things then started to deteriorate quickly. That's when the really hard stuff started. There wasn't anything I would say about John that I wouldn't say in front of him, and I believe he felt the same. We were a team getting through this. We didn't hide from each other. We talked openly to each other and to other people about what was going on. It wasn't necessary to share every last detail with our friends and family, but there is no shame in being sick. It was just he hand he was dealt.

John's family came over one Sunday afternoon for dinner in early summer 2024. His brothers, sisters-in-law, his son, and my mother were all at the house. John and I talked that week and decided since everyone would be over, we would have a family meeting. One of John's brothers and one of his sisters-in-law were retired. The other brother and sister-in-law were still working but could sometimes work remotely. We decided we needed some help. John's pain and condition had gotten worse. John's mind was still sharp. He was just very limited and needed help with virtually everything. I could leave the house for a few minutes, but he might need pain meds or bathroom assistance. Nights were challenging when John's pain was particularly acute. Maybe it was because there wasn't any other stimulus to distract him. For months, I slept with one ear and one eye open, getting up whenever John needed something. For a while, he started sleeping without pants so if he needed to get up and go to the bathroom, he wouldn't have to call to me. I rarely slept because I was constantly on call. The work load and the sleep deprivation were taking its toll on me. John and I both knew I needed some backup.

That day at the family meeting I told everyone we needed help. I said if they couldn't help us, we would hire someone to come in. It wasn't possible for me to stay with John 24 hours a day. They each volunteered to take a day of the week so I could go to my office or see friends or go to the dry cleaners. It was so helpful for me. It was a blessing for John. John cherished those days with his family, and they were happy to contribute. Occasionally, one of his brothers would come and stay with John for a night or two so I could go to the river house. Neither John nor I wanted to burden his family, but they were more than willing to step up. During that time, we also had friends who would come for a visit with John so I could leave. I appreciated everyone who put their lives on hold to be present for John and help me those last few months. They each talk about what a pleasure it was to get to spend those last months with John. For them, it wasn't a burden. It was a gift. And it was a gift for John.

Toothbrushing

As John's condition deteriorated his last six months, a little panic started to set in for me. John was becoming more and more dependent. He ate on his own for a few weeks. Then I started having to feed him. I had to give him all of his medications. I blew his nose. I cut his nails. I washed him. I cleaned his glasses. For the life of me, I never understood how John's glasses could get so dirty when he couldn't touch them. His days of relative independence were gone.

A huge challenge was brushing his teeth. It doesn't sound hard, but brushing someone else's teeth is not an easy task. I held the electric toothbrush in his mouth, and he tried to communicate with me through a series of grunts and head motions where he wanted me to brush. When you brush your own teeth, you stand in front of the mirror, hold your toothbrush, and do your thing. When I brushed John's teeth, I stood to one side of him and tried to move the toothbrush around his mouth. It's not a natural task. One of the first evenings I attempted the chore, we stood at the sink. He tried to motion with his head where he wanted me to brush. Then he moved and turned his head. Neither of us knew what the hell we were doing, and he started slowly rotating his body in a circle. I followed along beside him. Finally, we got to about one hundred and eighty degrees, and I said, "I think we can probably get this done without turning in circles." He immediately burst out laughing and spit toothpaste all over the bathroom wall. Guess who cleaned up that mess? The guy with two functional arms. We just had to laugh through it all.

Man Down

*John, at the Missouri Botanical
Garden, Summer, 2024
(photo by Mary)*

In July of that last summer, Badass Mary came up from Tennessee for ten days to help around the house and with John. His health was starting to get just a little worse each day. Friends and family would ask me, "How's John?" That summer I began telling them, "Today is his best day. Tomorrow will be his next best day." Mary told me during that summer visit that she finally understood what I meant. John wasn't getting better ever. I knew he was declining, and I was on a rollercoaster ride. But even though I knew things weren't good, I had no idea how bad they were. I had no idea just how close he was to the end. How do you know? Instead of worrying, I just knew that every day I needed to get up, get him his meds, get him fed, and keep him comfortable. When Mary went home in mid-July, she immediately booked a flight for the end of August with plans to stay two weeks through mid-September. She knew.

The last two weeks Mary was in St. Louis in September were a tremendous help to both John and me. She helped with the day-to-day, but she could also give input on how to settle the chaos. She had taken care of her mother who died of cancer. She had taken care of her father who died of cancer. She had taken care of her mother-in-law as she was failing. She took care of my dying father. Mary was an invaluable resource to have around. The two weeks she was in St. Louis, John started losing the feeling in his legs. He became very unstable, and we started putting him in the wheelchair to get around. At first, he could still get up and down and in and out of the chair, but he didn't trust himself to walk. Sometimes we held on to him as he walked, but more and more, we put him in the wheelchair. The house we designed was ideal for a wheelchair, even though we had had no idea it would come in handy. We had wide hallways and doors and a "roll-in shower" without the impediment of a door.

Because John didn't have the use of his arms, whenever he got up from a sitting position, he only had his legs to work with. The only way up was with his quads and glutes, which were strong. The sofa sat relatively low. When John got up, he would position his feet at a wider stance and pop right up in one quick motion. He had no other choice. Mom used to call John her "Jack in the Box."

One afternoon, I was with John in the living room, and he said he needed to go to the bathroom. As he popped up, he teetered over onto the floor. He wasn't hurt. It wasn't a bad fall. John was a big man, 6'0", and even sick, he weighed one hundred and seventy pounds. He couldn't use his arms to push himself up off the floor. And I couldn't lift him up. Mary was in the kitchen on the other side of the house. John's family is the loud family. My family isn't, so in a cool, calm voice with no hint of panic, I raised my tone just a bit and said, "Mom, could you come in here for a second, please?" She said she knew immediately; the calmness of my voice alerted her. She got to the living room, and the next fifteen minutes were like Lucy and Ethel trying to pick Fred off the floor. It was a complete sitcom episode that lasted the full thirty minutes. We couldn't lift him. At one point we considered trying to sit him on a 1' x 6' board to try to lift him up. We thought maybe we could get him on a footstool and tip him onto the sofa. That was the solution that finally worked. But we ended up pushing him face first right into the couch, knocking his glasses askew and sending them sliding half off of his face. John had a great sense of humor. He had to have a sense of humor to put up with Mary and me. It's not that my family is disrespectful, but we find humor in situations that most people wouldn't exactly find funny. We couldn't stop laughing. He wasn't mad at us, and we apologized abundantly. He also knew we were just doing the best we could. We were trying to keep him comfortable and safe. And we knew he was just trying to do the best he could trying to stay alive. After that fall, I began to put my arms around John's waist or under his arms and, with what leg strength he had to help, lift him out of the bed or chair and lower him into his wheelchair. It was too big of a risk to let him stand or sit on his own any longer.

Last Days

John's last week was difficult on everyone. Mom and I pushed him around from room to room in the wheelchair, and I would make the transfer to put him in the bed, the chair, or on the toilet. We had to be cautious getting him up and down because the muscles in his right shoulder had been inoperable since his surgery and had been deteriorating from nonuse for almost three years. His shoulder muscles were unable to hold his arm in the socket, so he started wearing a sling. At first, he wore a Walgreens sling, but then he was fitted for a custom sling that strapped to his midsection and held the arm into the socket. It was very uncomfortable for him, and he hated wearing it. He wasn't sure if the strapped-on sling or the shoulder pain was worse. It was a case of choosing one of two terrible options, neither of which would alleviate the pain. Whenever we needed to move John, any sudden movement around that shoulder could result in searing pain.

John had an oncology appointment on Thursday, and earlier that week, he told me he was going to tell his oncologist he wanted to stop treatment and go on hospice. For months, maybe years, John knew he was going to die. The decision to stop treatment was one he didn't take lightly. I see older people running and walking in the park. I see people pushing their workouts at the gym. We have been told to eat our Wheaties. Really, we are all just trying to do anything we can to stay alive, stay healthy, and try to be productive. John and I talked about wanting to honor the gift of life while still being able to contribute to those he loved and the world around him. He still wanted to be part of this life. He just didn't want to be immobile and incapacitated.

Mary left the Thursday morning that John had his oncology appointment. I wheeled him to my small truck, lifted him up, turned him around, and got him into the passenger seat. I folded up the wheelchair and threw it in the bed of the truck. Off we went to the hospital. Off Mary went to the airport. Cancer appointments seem to last for days. No one wants to be there. Treatments and doctors get backed up. Sometimes appointments run late because of emergencies. A 9:00 a.m. appointment can seem to last all day. We arrived at the appointment, and John got his blood drawn, per usual. A blood panel was always done to ensure John had enough red and white blood cells and platelets to receive chemo. We waited for a couple of hours, and John finally got called into a patient room. For some odd reason that day, John's current nurse, the physician assistant, and John's previous nurse were all there. John was particularly fond of his previous nurse who had recently been transferred to another department. It seemed like a cancer reunion party. He got to catch up with his entire care team.

When his oncologist came in the room, John told her that he was losing feeling in his legs and having trouble walking. This was the first time his doctor had seen him arrive at an appointment in a wheelchair. He told her he had taken a fall. He then indicated to her that he wanted to stop chemotherapy and be put in hospice care. The doctor asked him questions about how long these new symptoms had been going on, how much he was able to walk, and how stable he was. She told him she was supportive of him ceasing chemo and starting hospice. However, she mentioned that these new symptoms had appeared very quickly, and she couldn't be sure the symptoms were caused by the cancer. She indicated there was a possibility he could have an infection. She said, "I am fine with you going on hospice care. You are in charge of your own health. But what would you say if we put you in the hospital for a couple of days to run some tests? We could confirm you don't have something else going on that's causing the immobility. We could also do another MRI to take a look at your neck to see if there is any increased growth there." John really didn't want to go into the hospital. He and I and the doctor talked it over. The oncologist thought he would only be in the hospital for one day, two at the most. She said he would be there only long enough to get some test results. I thought it was reasonable to get some answers before making the decision to stop chemo. John reluctantly agreed. The doctor left to make some calls while we continued visiting with his care team. The oncologist came back and told us there wasn't a bed available. She said she would order a bed, send John home, and the hospital would call us when a bed became available. I loaded John back in the truck, and home we went.

It was a long day destined to get longer. I probably fed John when we got home, but I'm not completely certain about that. Around 7:00 p.m., our trusty nurse friend Ana stopped by to say "hi." It wasn't unusual for Ana to pop in. She had been a constant presence throughout John's cancer journey. We explained that the doctor wanted to run some tests, and we told her John was waiting on a bed on the oncology floor. Around 8:30 p.m., John said he needed to go to the restroom. I went over to the recliner to help pick him up to get him in the wheelchair. His legs were like rubber bands, and I couldn't hold him up. He didn't fall, but I just eased him onto the floor. Thank goodness Ana was there. She was always our angel's voice of reason. I thought back to when Mary and I had to get him off the floor. That day, he still had a little strength in his legs. While it wasn't easy, we shoved him up onto the sofa and then got him into the wheelchair. There wasn't a chance of that this time. There was no way for Ana and me to get him off the floor. Sometimes, logic doesn't show up during a crisis. My only solution was to call some of our neighbors to help get him up.

Ana provided the day's sanity. She told us we needed to call 911 and have the paramedics come. The paramedics are trained to help those who have fallen. She also thought they should go ahead and take him to the hospital. John was really against that idea. He didn't want didn't want to go to the hospital, and he didn't want a paramedics scene. I said, "Listen, when a bed opens, you're going to the hospital anyway. You might as well go now and wait on a bed there. Then, I won't have to get you there by myself." I thought that if he didn't go now, I'd be calling a transport later anyway. He finally agreed and asked if the paramedics could turn off their lights and siren because this wasn't an "emergency," and he didn't want to bother the neighbors. I told him, "Sorry. They won't do that."

The EMTs showed up. John was his normal, affable, talkative self. One of them told John what a "cool" space we lived in and how he loved our art. My anxiety was sky high while John and the paramedics were chatting about the oil paintings. It was fairly surreal. The paramedics got him up on the gurney, wheeled him out, and put him in the back of the ambulance. One of my neighbors later told me they saw John getting taken out of the house, but he was alert and seemed to be having a nice conversation. Yes, that was our John. The neighbor told me he didn't think it was too serious because John was acting normal. Ana told me to pack one bag for me and one for John. She told me not to rush, because he would have some time with the intake process. Ana thought we might be waiting for a while before he got to a room.

I took a deep breath. I didn't rush, but I didn't tarry gathering some essentials. The hospital is a big system of buildings that sits on four city blocks. Parking is at one end of the complex, and the emergency room is in the middle of the complex. I probably walked a couple of city blocks or more within the hospital to get to the ER. When I got there, the receptionist said, "Oh, John's been waiting for you." They immediately had taken him back to a room. I suspect it was because his oncologist had already placed the order for him to be admitted, and he was already waiting for an oncology room. Initially, John wasn't taken to the cancer floor. He was still in the Emergency Department, but he had a private "area" with a curtain. The parade of doctors, nurses, residents, and housekeepers began their rounds. Everyone seemed to ask him and me the same questions over and over. It was exhausting, and it went on throughout the night. Around midnight, a resident came in and asked John when he had last urinated. He said he was trying to go to the bathroom when he fell, and it had probably been about eight hours. The doctor suggested they insert a catheter. It wasn't at all what John wanted. But I told him that I couldn't get him up to go to the bathroom, and it would be hard for me to roll him over to pee in the container. He reluctantly agreed. A nurse catheterized him, and when it was inserted, he discharged a copious amount of liquid. John had lost feeling in his lower body, and he couldn't feel an urge to go to the bathroom.

I consider myself a realistic optimist. Or maybe I'm just stupid. In hindsight, it is likely John's inability to urinate and the amount of urine he discharged signaled his bladder was failing. It was a flashing red sign that his condition was deteriorating. As he stayed in the Emergency Department, he had more tests run. Doctors came in all night. At one point the next morning, one of the nurses brought him a sandwich of some sort. John said he wasn't hungry, but I fed him half of it. They also had him on medication drips. He would occasionally ask for a pain pump shot, but not very often. He was alert but seemed tired. His voice was weak. Sometimes he would say something, and I would have to get up and go over to the bed to get close to him to hear what he was saying. He was dying. And I had no clue. I mean, I knew he was dying. He had been dying for three years. But I didn't know he was slipping away right then. I figured his pain meds were making him weak and drowsy. At some point on Friday, the day after he went to the hospital, I asked one of the doctors if he had an infection. The doctor shook his head and told us, "No." John was still on a waiting list for an oncology room, and he was still waiting on an MRI test to determine if the cancer mass had grown.

As Friday wore on, John mostly slept. I had called John's brothers that morning and told them John was in the hospital. In the early afternoon, John asked one of the doctors if they would call hospice. A few hours later, a nurse came in and said a palliative care doctor was on her way down. I had just a few weeks earlier expressed my displeasure with their service and told the department head what a dismal experience we had with their care. I looked over at John and said, "Oh, shit." He gave me a weak smile and kind of chuckled. A palliative physician and a social worker, neither of whom we had met, came into John's room. They were very kind and professional. They asked John if he needed anything, and he, again, said he wanted hospice care. When they were leaving, I walked out with them and asked them in the hallway if they knew John had previously been in palliative care. They looked at each other, and the doctor said, "Yeah. We were nervous about coming down here." I said that I appreciated what they did for people, and I hoped our situation was unusual. They asked me if I needed anything. I said, "Yes. John's oncologist thought he might have an infection, and that's why he came to the hospital. I've been told he doesn't have an infection. He's waiting on an MRI and will then get discharged. I don't know how I'm going to get him home." The social worker said, "How did he get here?" I told them that I had called the paramedics yesterday evening, but earlier in the day when he had his oncology appointment, I put him in a wheelchair and brought him to his appointment in my truck. I said, "But I don't think I'm going to be able to get him home, now." In the moment it didn't register with me, but one of them said, *"You put him in your truck and brought him here yesterday?"* I said, "Yes. And I also have no idea where to get a hospital bed when he comes home. Can you help me with that?" I guess no one knows when it's the end, or maybe health professionals aren't allowed to say. I imagine the palliative team was thinking, *What are you talking about? He's not going home.*

Just after the palliative team left, John's brother Ken and his sister-in-law, Linda, came to the hospital. They suggested I go home for a bit. John's other brother Kevin was on site at the hospital undergoing his own chemo. His first round of treatment had begun two days earlier. He had planned on coming down to the ER to see John when his own treatment was wrapped up for the day. When Ken suggested I leave for a while, I agreed it would be wise for me to go home and get some sleep. John was scheduled for his MRI at 8:00 p.m., and it would take several hours. Kevin said he would stay with John until they took him for his test. I would come back to the hospital while John was in the MRI, and I would be there when he got back to the room. John's son, Liam, worked nights. As I was on my way home that afternoon, I called Liam and told him his dad was in the hospital. I remember telling him, "You are absolutely welcome to come, but this is not an emergency. They are going to run an MRI test, and I think they will probably send him home tomorrow."

I went home. I fell asleep. I set my alarm for 7:30 p.m. so I could get up and go back to the hospital. Right after I got up, I got a call from Kevin saying John had finally gotten onto the oncology floor. He also said his MRI was delayed. Kevin said he would stay and call me when they wheeled him out for the test. After a couple of hours, I reached back out to Kevin and told him I was on my way over. Kevin had been at the hospital for the last three days for his own treatment, and he needed to go home and get some rest, too. He stayed until I got to the swanky palatial oncology room: a very nice private room with a sofa and a chair. Kevin left about 10:00 p.m. John was mostly sleeping, but we talked some with questions like, "How are you feeling? Do you need anything?" He asked me to put lip balm on his lips. Even before John got sick, John always had a lip balm tube in his pocket. Around 11:30 p.m. an orderly came into the room and rolled John out to his MRI.

I fell asleep in the room's recliner. Around 2:30 a.m., my phone rang. I hadn't slept in days. Actually, I hadn't slept in months, maybe years. Even though my phone was beside me, I woke up just as it stopped ringing. I didn't recognize the missed call number. Things were hazy. It was the middle of the night. Almost immediately, the phone rang again, and I picked up. The voice on the other end of the phone said, "Is this William, John's partner?" I said, "Yes." She said, "This is blah-blah from blah-blah." I have no recollection of her name or the department. She kept talking: "John's heart blah-blah. Blah-blah CPR and we have blah-blah." I remember saying, "I'm sorry. What?" She said again, "John's heart stopped on the MRI table. We did CPR and have taken him to the Intensive Care Unit." She continued, saying, "Someone will come to his room and take you to him." I hung up. Dazed.

The oncology floor nurse who had been in and out a few times that night came into the room and asked me if someone had called me. I told her yes, and she said she would take me to the ICU. She had to find someone to help us get there across the campus' four blocks. She said she didn't know how to get there through all the nonpublic hallways and tunnels. It seemed like we walked forever. But they finally got me to the ICU department. By this time, it was 3:00 a.m. I walked into the room, and there were probably a dozen people there. I suspect they were nurses, doctors, residents, and lawyers. The radiology physician was the only one who spoke. She told me that during his MRI, John's heart stopped. They did CPR, got his heart beating again, gave him medication to stabilize his blood pressure, intubated him, and put him on a breathing machine. She said the medical staff did not realize he had a "Do Not Resuscitate" order until after they stabilized him. She then asked me if I wanted them to remove him from life support. I was stunned.

I think I asked a few questions like, "If you remove the support, how long will he live?" I think she said she didn't know, but it could be minutes or days. I'm not sure what else I asked or said. I told them, "Keep him on life support for now. I'll call his son and brothers in a few hours. They will want to come down, and we can make that decision together." After I told her that, she said something that struck me at the time as completely bizarre. She said, "He almost got through the MRI test. I can check to see if we can see anything from the images and get you the results." I remember saying, "We're not going to need those results."

In those early morning hours in the ICU, the doctors assured me he was on "comfort care." He had an IV with pain and relaxation medications to make him comfortable. They guaranteed me he wasn't in any pain. As the hospital staff filed out of the room, one of the nurses told me I could stay the night in the recliner. I looked at John. There wasn't any doubt in my mind he was gone. His chest moved up and down from the breathing machine. But there was no sign of life. He wasn't there. He was lying on an air mattress of some kind. I sat on the side of the bed, and an alarm sounded. I panicked a little and immediately stood up and went over to the recliner. Maybe I wasn't supposed to be on the bed with him. In hindsight, I think it was an alert for the nurse if he was falling out of the bed. I just thought I wasn't supposed to be sitting there. I sat in the chair. I didn't cry.

I guess I didn't cry because for three years I had been waiting for this day. I knew it would eventually come. I had already been crying for years. Or maybe I didn't cry because I was in shock. I sat in the chair. I dozed in and out and, around 8:00 a.m., I began calling immediate family to explain what happened. Probably an hour later, John's son, his brothers, sisters-in-law, nieces, and nephews started showing up in the ICU. His family had as much time as they wanted with him in the room. I was there throughout most of those visits.

John, painting with his good hand during Chester kitchen remodel, August 2022

That's when I cried. I cried because I knew how much John meant to all of us.

Around 11:30 a.m., Liam, Kevin, Ken and I collectively agreed it was time to pull life support. I collected John's family from the waiting room and the hallway, and we gathered in the ICU room. I told the nurse they could call the pulmonologist to remove the breathing tube. Around ten minutes later, the doctor came in, stopped the blood pressure medication, turned off the breathing machine, and removed John's tube. A few minutes later, surrounded by his family the color drained from his face and John stopped breathing.

The Calls

To this day, I don't know how or why John died. Of course, I know he had Ewing Sarcoma. But I don't really understand why his heart stopped. I understand a heart attack. I understand a gun shot. I understand a car accident. I understand old age when a person's organs and body are weakened. In the last six months, John's scans showed he had cancer spots on his lungs. They weren't big, and the doctor wasn't too worried about them. I understand lung cancer when you can't breathe anymore. Allegedly John's organs were strong. And the doctor told him over and over in his appointments that his body was strong. I just don't understand what killed him. His death certificate reads, "Cause of Death: Advanced Ewing Sarcoma." But how did that kill him? Our nurse friend Ana supposes the tumor on his spine started cutting off circulation, blood flow, and function to his organs. Maybe that makes sense. Ultimately, it doesn't matter. I just can't make total sense of it.

After they removed life support, the hospital staff told us we could stay as long as we liked. I didn't have a problem with his dead body. John wasn't there. That was a shell. I was in my father's room after he died. I was called next door when I was in my early twenties when my grandmother died. I helped the coroner put her in the body bag. I guess I have a tolerance for death. But none of us felt the need to linger afterward. His family had already been with him for a couple of hours. There wasn't a need to stay with his body. John's nieces from Indianapolis had been called, and they were on their way, a four-hour drive. But after a few hours gathered at the hospital, we all made the decision to go ahead and pull support even though they hadn't arrived yet. John had a "do not resuscitate" order and had said many, many times he did not want to be kept alive. It was difficult knowing he was in the very position that he expressly indicated he did not want to be in. While his nieces didn't make it to the hospital, they came back to our house that afternoon. Honestly, I'm glad they didn't see him lying lifeless in that bed. That's not how I want them to remember him. I want them to remember him as vibrant and funny and full of life.

I started packing up the few belongings I had brought to the ICU room. One of the incredibly kind nurses came in and handed me three empty tubes that looked like vials that would hold drawn blood. He didn't tell me what they were for, but I conjectured they could hold John's ashes. Taped to the tubes was a print-out of John's EKG heartbeat. It was an amazing and beautiful sentiment. I knew there wouldn't be ashes in those vials since John had donated his body. I gave the EKG vials to John's son, Liam, and each of his brothers. Liam is a metal fabricator. That fall, he fabricated what looked like an "old-school" desk nameplate and etched John's name, year of birth, and year of death into it. He then laser cut John's EKG heartbeat above his name. John's heartbeat nameplate was our special Christmas gift that year.

The staff asked me to go to the ICU waiting room. They were gathering paperwork for me to sign. I sent his family to my house while I waited for the papers. While in the waiting room, I called some of our close friends and family. If I could get through those handfuls of calls, I would ask them to let other people know. Those calls were the hardest conversations I've ever had to have. I was physically, emotionally, and spiritually exhausted. I knew each of the people I called would be devastated. They knew John had been in the hospital. But according to me, I was working on getting him a hospital bed for when he came home. Maybe I was the only one who didn't know he wasn't coming home. Or possibly I convinced them, too. I don't know if they were shocked. I just tried to get through each conversation without breaking down. I think I used the tired line I've used over and over since then. I probably said, "I'm sorry for us. But I'm relieved for him. Nobody deserves to go through that." And those words are true. Dying is part of living, and I am sorry for us. But it was still a devastating goodbye.

John, still wobbly from surgery and using a cane, enjoying sunshine one afternoon after treatment, March 2022

Announcing Death in the 21st Century

The death announcement used to be so easy. There were rules. You wrote an obituary and placed it in the local paper. It's not like that anymore. I've thought many times in the recent past how crass the Facebook death post is. It just doesn't seem right or respectful to me. Obviously, John's family knew of his passing. We called or told close friends, and they called other friends. But almost no one reads "the paper" anymore. Most of our friends who are our age are on Facebook. If we were 30 years old, I might have put the announcement on Instagram or TikTok or Snapchat. After everyone had called close friends and family, the next day on Sunday morning, I swallowed hard and wrote on Facebook:

Hello everyone. It's Bill, John's partner. John left us yesterday after battling Ewing Sarcoma for more than 3 years. While our light today is a little dimmer, and our life today has a little less joy, please know that it is a blessing that John is no longer in pain. Especially for the last 6 months, John was in excruciating physical pain. It was an honor and a gift to be with him even through the pain. And even in his most difficult moments, he never lost his sense of humor or his gratitude for those around him.

He and I are extremely grateful for all the kind words of support, the prayers, and all the good energy coming our way. John had some human angels, and there aren't words to express how grateful I am for those of you and how you touched his and my life. His life was better because of you, and I learned so much from you about how and what to do. I appreciate all the meals. It made things so much easier. And thank you for checking in again and again even when I told you not to bring anything because he was too sick to eat. You checked the next day, then the next, and then the next until he could eat. Thanks for the cards, letters, and little tokens to make him smile. Oddly for me, thanks to those who brought flowers. I never really thought much about flowers, but when he was lying in bed, he could look at the windowsill and see something beautiful. Thank you for inviting us to things even when we declined over and over. And maybe on the 9th invitation, we could show up. But mostly, thank you for all the kindness these past three years.

Even though it may be impossible, John wouldn't want you to be sad. He would want you to tip a glass of bourbon, sip a glass of wine, or raise a glass of sparkling water to a life full of joy, happiness, and togetherness. Godspeed.

Of course, the next few days were a blur. Mid-week, I was with Ana. I handed her my phone and said, "'Heart' all these comments for me, would you?" I didn't want to read them. I just wanted to escape. Later on, I read the wonderful sentiments. In the days afterward, though, I just wanted the world to go dark. I didn't want to be seen or heard.

The Body

After everyone left our house the day John passed away, I went to bed and slept eleven hours. John had donated his body to the Washington University Medical School. Because his cancer was so rare in adults, he really wanted his body to be a learning tool for others. The hospital where John died was part of the Washington University education system. The morning he died, I told the nurses in the ICU about John's donation. They said someone would contact me. Over the next several days there was a series of phone calls and emails regarding his donation. I talked to the Office of Decedent Affairs several times. I sent them the acceptance letter for John's body. They told me to reach out to the body donation program, and they would instruct me on how to proceed. One problem was that John had died on a weekend, and when I called the program, I had to leave a message on someone's voicemail. Monday afternoon, I got another call from the hospital asking me what I wanted them to do with the body. I said to the nice lady on the phone, "Look. I don't care what you do with him. Don't send him here, and don't charge me for storage." Maybe this is normal death chaos.

In the literature John received along with his donation acceptance letter, it stated that his family would be responsible for having the body transported to Washington University's donation program. At the time, we Googled how much it cost to transport a body. It was around $600. John said, "Do you think they'd take me if you just put me in the back of your truck?" I laughed and said, "My guess is no." After multiple calls and emails over several days, someone finally told me that the body storage facility was not at the hospital even though it was all part of the same system. I figured they would just move him from the eighth floor down to the basement. Apparently, the storage warehouse is offsite. Six hundred dollars later they stopped calling me.

Chocolate Chip Cookies

I woke the morning of September 15th after those eleven hours of dead, dreamless sleep to a dreary, cloudy, drizzly day. How could it not be a miserable day? I looked out the glass sliding door to see a gray plastic container soaked in rain sitting on the patio step. There was a card on top. The writing was blurred, ink smeared. The container was filled with chocolate chip cookies. When our friend Sean feels helpless, he bakes chocolate chip cookies. It's the only thing he can cook. I opened the card and tried to decipher the message. Sean's wet, sorrowful, muddied note was smeared by his tears, my tears, and heaven's tears. The whole world was crying with me.

The Return of A.J.

About six months after John died, I got a text from our Japanese artist friend, A.J., that said, "Hi, Bill. How have you been with John, Sue, and Jen? I'm still jumping." He also included two links to very impressive "short" films. One was set in Tower Grove Park, just half a block from my house. It featured portraits that he had painted, and they faded in and out with the park in the background. The second video featured his abstract art pieces fading in and out with a beach and the surf in the background. Of course, both films showed him jumping rope on the beach and in the park. He is a true artist.

I responded to his text, "Hi A.J. Love the films! I still see Jen and Sue but the cancer got John and he left us in Sept. While an interesting idea, we didn't have his body dissected in half and displayed in a museum! That's your project! I'll share your films with Sue and Jen. They'll love them. Hope all is well!" After A.J. expressed his condolences, I wrote back, "Thanks so much. It was a rough few months. But John kept smiling until the end. And he loved your visit. Keep jumping and we'll try to get everyone together one day soon."

Adjustment

I had a life before John. I had a life after we met. We had a life together that that worked for us. Then I had a life of caregiving. I will transition into a life without John. I will have new adventures. I will meet new friends. I don't know when I'll become single instead of being widowed. I expect that to happen at some point. I recently had dinner with John's brother, Ken. He asked me if I was dating anyone. I was shocked. It wasn't a question I ever anticipated anyone asking me. In hindsight, he may have asked the question to indicate to me that it would be okay whenever that happens.

Our lives morph because our human experience constantly changes. There are friends of John's and mine that I rarely see anymore. John's sickness and death journey put us in a different physical space and a different emotional space. I may not be as close to some older friends, but that creates a space for new friends and new explorations. If I become close to those old friends again, that creates an opportunity to generate something new with them.

Recently, I was in my front yard watering the plants. One of my neighbors stopped by and told me he misses seeing me sit out front with John. He misses seeing us work in the yard. I miss that, too. I've had the opportunity to spend consecutive days with close family and friends. Those days are still so difficult. I need to hold it together so they think I'm okay and nothing's wrong. Nothing is wrong. But there is still a lot that isn't right. My drive to reconnect with the world hasn't returned yet. My tank hasn't been replenished.

John, left, and me during kitchen remodel, March 2021

I finished all the work on Mary's house, and I listed it for sale. I spend as much time in Chester as I can. John would like that. Since John died, I don't cook much anymore. I'll make a sandwich. Or I'll throw something easy together. Or I'll have raw vegetables and cheese for dinner. Or I'll get carryout. I used to love to cook. Or maybe I just thought I loved to cook. I used to think it was a creative outlet for me. But maybe I only liked to cook when there was someone to feed. I never craved the compliment. Sometimes what I cook isn't good. You hear the phrase, "made with love." Maybe I craved the love it elicited. That's gone. After the sign went up at Mary's house, I cooked shrimp and grits that weekend for dinner in Chester. It was an easy assignment. I've made it a million times. John always loved it. I hope to get my cooking groove back.

John's brother, Kevin, gets quarterly immunotherapy treatments for his Mantle Cell Lymphoma. His oncologist assured Kevin the chemotherapy regimen would enable remission. It did. He is cancer free. As confident as the doctor was that she would get Kevin in remission, she was equally confident that his cancer would come back in a few years. That chapter has yet to be written.

Death happens every day. Death happens to every family. Humans die in war. Humans die in accidents. Humans die from sickness and disease. Each death story is personal for those who were left behind heartbroken. There is no guidebook for dealing with struggle, hardship, and calamity. Everyone's tragedies are uniquely different. If we can recognize the presence of joy and growth and companionship in the face of adversity, maybe the struggle can be a gift.

"Vienna"

Each year, Washington University's medical and physical therapy students host a Donor Remembrance Ceremony to thank the family and friends of those that donated their bodies to the Washington University research departments. The ceremony to honor John and the others who donated was held in late April 2025.

I didn't particularly have a strong personal need to attend the ceremony. I appreciated the students' efforts, and I appreciated their gratitude. I didn't need the ceremony for closure. I didn't need the ceremony to make me feel better. But I did feel somewhat of an obligation to show up, particularly because I had invited all of John's family and some close friends. However, I did make it clear this wasn't an obligatory event. I wanted them to attend *only* if they wanted to come. The ceremony was also live-streamed on the Body Donor Program's website, and the video would be available afterward on the website.

There were four of us who attended the ceremony: John's brother, Kevin, our friends Ana and Sue, and me. My expectations for the event were low. I really only attended to support the others who wanted to go. Yet it was an amazingly well-planned, thoughtful, heartfelt, and beautiful event. Students gave tributes, performed live music, read original poetry and other pieces, and shared their experiences learning from our loved ones. It was moving, and I'm so grateful for their efforts to appreciate our gifts to them.

After short opening remarks, the program kicked off with a vocal and keyboard performance by an incredibly talented student. She sang and played a rendition of the song "Vienna," by Billy Joel. I could feel John's presence all around me. His spirit was there punking me, daring me not to laugh out loud. He *hated* Billy Joel. I heard his voice in my ear saying, "God. Turn that shit off."

Regrets

I have very few regrets. But I have them. It's natural to look back and ruminate on shortcomings or what you could have done better. I got up and did my best every day. Sometimes, though, your best might be less than what you would like. I regret not holding John more. I wish I had lain in bed with him more at night. The dishes or laundry could have waited. I regret getting off of his bed when he was on life support in the ICU when the alarm sounded the morning he died. I wish I had sat there and held his hand.

John's maternal family was from the East Coast. As a kid, his family would go back east. The church ladies in the Polish community would make homemade perogies. I regret never making him perogies. We talked about a short trip to Louisville to go on the Bourbon Trail. I regret we didn't make that trip.

Some people have a drug or alcohol addiction. I have an art collection habit. John would jokingly chastise me when I would haul in another painting that he thought was horrendous. In the last couple of months when John was declining, I bought a series of four paintings that needed restoration. I stuck them in the closet because I had bigger fish to fry at the time than art restoration: John was fighting to stay alive. *New art might be a distraction*, I thought. I regret I didn't share those paintings with him and give him a chance to "chastise" me one more time.

Especially toward the end, I was so spent. John would ask me to hold the tissues while he would blow his nose. He would ask me to put lotion on his legs. I did all the things he asked. I didn't complain. I regret not wanting to do them and not wanting to do them more.

I wasn't as vulnerable with John as I could have been. I didn't want to disappoint him or let him down. He didn't want to disappoint me, either. He carried on like a good mate. I carried on like a good captain, making sure the ship ran smoothly. I was strong. I regret sacrificing being authentically hurt and shattered with him.

I regret the last two hours I spent with John. I didn't know when they wheeled him away it would be the last time I would see him alive. I don't know that I would have done or said anything differently. But I regret not telling him I loved him one more time. Honestly, I may have told him I loved him before he was rolled away. I don't remember. I do remember telling him as I put lip balm on his lips, "I'll see you in a few hours. I'll be here when you get back."

Reminders

Many days I feel an overwhelming sense of guilt. I feel guilty that I didn't do enough, that I didn't make him comfortable enough. Sometimes I think I did it wrong. I couldn't keep him alive. But it may just be misplaced survivor's guilt. My guilt is rooted in the reality that John was the one who had to die. He was the good one. He was the kind one. He was the funny one. He was the one that everyone loved. He was the least deserving of death, let alone an excruciatingly painful one. He asked me on several occasions if I thought he was going to hell. He was already in hell, and so was I. But if John, whose being was pure love, is now in hell, there is no hope for any of us. We will all be there.

No matter what I did, I couldn't take John's pain away. I would have given anything to make him feel better. John loved me and his family and friends. The irony is John would be devastated knowing his death is the source of our pain and hurt and suffering as we carry on without him.

One evening, not long after John started chemo treatments, and I was just hitting my caregiving groove, I made dinner. His stomach was queasy. In addition to whatever protein I cooked, I made mashed potatoes. John loved mashed potatoes. I brought dinner over to John, and he innocently but seriously said, "You know, I think I'll have chips instead of potatoes." It took every ounce of willpower in me not to chuck a bag of Lay's right at his head. I clenched my jaw and reminded myself that it was a blessing John was upright and alive.

We laughed a lot about that over the next two and a half years. Now, whenever I see mashed potatoes on a menu, I smile and think of John.

The reminders of his story are everywhere for me. I'm reminded every day when I drive by the hospital on my commute to work. I'm reminded when I look in the closet and see leftover lidocaine cream. I'm reminded when I walk by the lilac John had me plant because it was his mom's favorite bush. I have visions of John sitting out on the patio in what he called "his urban oasis." I think of John every time I hear the word "stupid." John would call things "stupid delicious" and "stupid fun," or say that the weather was "stupid cold." I see John during the day with my eyes open. I see John at night with my eyes closed. I play the movie. And I replay the movie.

Besides John's cousins sponsoring a tree for him in Tower Grove Park, other friends gave me two trees when John passed away. One is a redbud that I planted in Chester. One is a flowering magnolia that I planted in St. Louis. I'm reminded of John every day when I see one of those three trees. I made a promise to my friends that I would keep those trees alive better than I was able to keep John alive.

Maybe there isn't an ending to this story. There is a ripple effect of who John was and how he affected those around him. John wasn't a perfect man. I have to be careful not to canonize him. But John did have and does have a perfect soul. People tell me, "I think about John all the time." But why? Are they missing John? Are they missing the idea of him? Are they mourning their own eventual deaths? For those who weren't around him for years, are they mourning the loss of the possibility of reconnecting with an old friend and establishing a deeper friendship? Simply, I think we are all grieving the loss of possibility.

John cared deeply for his little dot in the world. He loved his people. He loved his job. He loved his garden. He loved his son. He loved me. He loved his life. He just tried to take care of his little dot in the world. He hoped his love and care would be the spark of energy that would ignite the next person's little dot to be loved and cared for.

It's been a year since John passed away. Every time I cut the grass in Chester, I look up to the porch and see him there, ravaged by cancer, ravaged by chemo, ravaged by the fight. I see him watching me mow the lawn. I see him wanting to contribute to the project but unable to do so. I can't get that vision out of my head. It's heartbreaking. Some might say it's a ghost. It's not. It's just a daytime dream. Even though it's a difficult dream, I cherish it because I just don't want to forget.

John liked sitting upfront in the living room with the big open windows. He would see our neighbors and feel connected to the world. John enjoyed sitting outside in the front yard listening to music. He liked to putter in the front and side gardens and talk to people as they walked by. I don't sit upfront or in the front garden much anymore. I don't feel like connecting. That desire will return, I hope. John would want me to connect with our community.

I promised myself when John died that for the first year, I wouldn't do anything rash or abrupt. My personality lends itself to making big changes during bouts of chaos. I am prone to making a hard right, a hard left, or a U-turn. I committed not to quit my job, not to sell my house, not to move, and not to date. I've upheld that commitment for now. Year one was a lesson in survival. It was a test of my will to get up every day and go to work. It was a lesson in trying to live as normal a life as possible. In year two, I'm committed to trying to figure out what I want out of life. I don't think this experience changed the core of who I am. My values are the same as before. However, my perspective is different. My priorities are different. My goals are different. Year two will be a reflection and an assignment of learning to live a successful, happy, productive, and meaningful life. It will be a test of what I've learned though this journey with John.

Love, John

I won the lottery because John and I had twenty-one years together. I am so thankful for that. I am very aware that discovering your person and having that connection for over two decades is an enormous gift. I am a better person because of John. He trained me. I will sometimes do something and say, "That's not how John would have done it." And I'll do it over. I'll do it better. He trained me to slow down and do my best. He trained me to love in a way I never knew existed. I don't know what John would say to us now, but I think it might be this:

To Those I Have Left: Don't cry. I did all the things. I worked hard. I played hard. I loved hard. I saw the world. I did my best. I am so grateful for all you did for me in my journey of life. I was blessed to have a son I love more than life itself. I was blessed to have an amazing partner. I was blessed to be surrounded by family and friends who loved me and wanted to see me happy and who just wanted to see my pain go away. You supported me. You cared for me. You fed me stupid delicious food. You hugged me. You kissed me. You sat with me. You brought me "treats." My wish is you take that love for me and extend it to others. Give it to the others that you don't love so much. Don't bicker. Don't fight. Every day is a gift. Every person you encounter is created with God's love. You have something to offer to everyone on this planet. And every person can offer you something. Let others teach you. Show your love. Give your love. Receive that love from others. Be kind. Be respectful. You don't have to agree. But agree to love others. Agree to grow from others. Agree to learn from others. Agree to learn and grow and love until you take your last breath. We never know the impact we have on others. The one small stone plopped in the water can create a wave far away. We don't know what or who is on the other side feeling our wave. Make your wave count. Make your wave positive. Make your energy a powerfully good current that is a force for more of God's amazing creation. Everyone has a story. We all learn from these stories. Share your story. Tell your story. Sing your story. Draw your story. Express your story. Live your story. Love your story. The two most momentous occasions are when we arrive in this world and when we leave this world. I was shrouded in love when I arrived, and I was shrouded in love when I left. You made me feel like I was the luckiest man in the world. Thank you for your contribution to my life. Thank you for your love. Love, John

Epilogue

Why did I write *Love, John*? The answer is multi-faceted. Partially, this narrative may be an antidote for grief. I suppose it's some form of therapy to ease my anxiety. The writing makes the story seem real and not just a dream. But it's more than that. There are many important people that have lived before us. There are Presidents that I know nothing about. But if I were interested, I could find their writings and research their lives. John's life and death was unique. His life wasn't necessarily extraordinary like a President's. But John's life means something to those of us still here. Fifteen months after John's death, John's niece welcomed a baby boy with the middle name John. The new John deserves to know his namesake. The new John needs to know his great-uncle's story.

All of us have our own remarkable story. In two hundred years, someone may find John's. Will the humanity story be the same hundreds and thousands of years later? Will thoughts and attitudes on living, dying, and death evolve? Will the concepts of commitment, love, and loss change? Can anyone learn from this writing? The billions of souls that have shown up and left us have had their own human journey. Maybe someone reading this will gain some insight into our shared humanity. My journey is shaped by where I sit in the stands. Each person has a different seat. Each person sees something different. Each person feels something different. Each person experiences something different. By sharing our stories, we gain a glimpse into a different worldview. By seeing another angle, we gain an opportunity for growth.

John and I had projects. We partnered. We owned a business. We designed a house. We rehabbed the Chester house. We bought a building, and we sold a building. I didn't want the partnership to end. If John were here, he'd roll his eyes and shake his head at my book-writing project. He'd say, "Of course you're writing a book. Can't you just chill out for a little while?" Then he'd jump in and help. I wrote because this is my last project with John.

John had many friends because he was easy to love. His and my friends and family deserve to know his story. Many were, and are, reluctant to ask the questions. The story is difficult. The story has a difficult ending. They deserve to know.

This narrative shows a glimpse into John's life journey and what he endured. This narrative expresses a glimpse into our life, and it gives a glimpse into my life after John left. This narrative describes a harrowing but loving story. This narrative explains a

John, enjoying a margarita, July 2018

side of John and me that most people don't know. There are many thousands of people grieving their own "John." Maybe these stories will touch them, and they, for a short moment, will know they aren't alone in their pain.

The vulnerability of writing this narrative is extremely unsettling. I'm supposed to be strong. I'm supposed to be unwavering. This story exposes my sadness, my weaknesses, and my heartbreak. I know it's okay (and healthy) to be sad, weak, and heartbroken. But knowing it's okay doesn't eliminate the discomfort. Yet discomfort creates space for growth, and discomfort is a painful but necessary ingredient for healing.

I have a job. I have projects that are now solely mine. Those things fill my days. Nights and weekends are eerily silent. I don't mind the silence. It's not exactly lonely, because my thoughts are always with John. But there is a lot of quiet time to explore my thoughts, explore my feelings. Frankly, I wrote to help heal my soul.

I wrote because I don't want to forget, and I don't want others to forget. I wrote because I don't want John's story to die. We didn't have a wake after John died, but maybe this is the memorial we all needed. I know it's the memorial I needed.

John, right, and me on the Chester porch, October 2023